## Introduction

This is a collection of the "Down de Bayou" series numbers one through five of the continuing adventures of two bestest and lifelong friends, Cajuns named Boo and Tib. Boo is the nickname for Boudreaux and Tib is for Thibodaux.

I began writing, creating, borrowing, cloning these jokes in October of 2009. I created the facebook page "Down de Bayou" shortly afterwards and began posting a joke a day ever since. The jokes in this collection were first posted in the later part 2009 through 2011. Go "Like" us on facebook to receive your daily Boo and Tib joke.

Look for more editions of "Down de Bayou" at your friendly Kindle store soon.

...Med Magill

Many thanks to my dear wife Wendy, our two beautiful children Molly and Trent, relatives, and friends for tolerating my jokes...Bon chance

1

Tib: Hey Boo, you knows de differance between de erotic and de kinky?

Boo: Why no? Watt bees de differance?

Tib: Well, wit one you uses a feather, wit de utter, you uses de whole chicken.

2

Tib: Can you believes dat Congress done passes dat stimulus bill, dat book explainin' it all wuz some 3 inches tick.

Boo: Ha, I wonders watt de 10 commandments would have looked like if Moses would have had to pass it by Congress.

3

Boo: Looks like de Wal Mart havin a Michael Jackson sale down dare.

Tib: Really, watts on sale?

Boo: Dey got boys pants half off.

4

Boo: Well, now dat de oldest boy be 16 now, Marie sez I gots to tell him bout de birds and de bees.

Tib: Boo, your boy been datin dat widow down de bayou for 3 years now, watt you goin to tell him?

Boo: I'm goin to tell him dat de birds and bees be doin de same ting.

5

Boo: Tib, did you know dat it sez here in de paper dat most Eskimos washes dare clothes it Tide.

Tib: Dat's obvious Boo, it be too cold out tide.

6

Disclaimer: Lord, may I apologize for the following joke in case it may have offend some people afflected with dyslexia. But then again, it's not like they going to be writin me or anything.

Boo: Tib, you know watt D.N.A. stands for?

Tib: Sure do my friend, dat is short for de National Dyslexics Association.

7

Tib: Dat cold you got still sounds bad.

Boo: Well I wents to see dat doctor you told me bout yesterday.

Tib: Good for you, watt he do for you?

Boo: Dat doctor told me to drinks a big ole glass of orange juice after a hot bath.

Tib: Sounds like good advice you know. Did it help you?

Boo: Don't know yet, I still haven't finished drinking de hot bath.

8

Boo: Tib, you know dis fishing trip for de las two days and three nights, and all dat gas and bait for just one fish, dat fish costed us 500 dollars.

Tib: Aye yi yi! it's a good ting we didn't catch two.

9

Boo: Hey Tib, sez here dat dare be 10 thousand battered women in dis state.

Tib: Watt? And I'm still eatin mine plain.

10

Boo: I axes de manager down at de plant today if I could gets tomorrow off so I could hep my Marie wit de cleanin of de house and garage.

Tib: Did you get de day off?

Boo: Nope. I knew I could counts on him.

## 11

Boo: I had de nicest dream las night. I dreamed dat I wuz gone fishin on dis beautiful bayou wit just me and a fishin pole.

Tib: I had a nice dream too. I dreams I wuz in bed wit these two beautiful women and passin a good time.

Boo: Tib, you dreams bout being wit two women and you don't calls your best friend Boo?

Tib: I did but your wife sez you done went fishin.

## 12

Boo: Man! Dat lightnin strike wuz close no?

Tib: You know dat de lightnin travels at 186 thousand miles a second.

Boo: Dat fast. Just tink how much faster it would be if it didn't zig zag so much.

## 13

Tib: There's one ting bout de speed of light.

Boo: Watts dat?

Tib: It gets here too early in de mornin.

## 14

Boo: Hey Mah ree, if I wuz to give you a thousand dollars minus 6 percent, how much would you take off?

Marie: Everyting but my ear rings.

## 15

Boo:  Last night I axes de wife if she wants some Super Sex.

Tib:  Watt did she say?

Boo:  She said she'd take de soup.

## 16

Tib:  Hey Boo, why you lookin so down today.

Boo:  You member Marie and me we got married when she wuz 16 and she done got pregnant. Her papa he give me de option to marry her rite den and dare or go prison for 20 years.

Tib:  Yep, I member dat. But dat a long time ago Boo. Why you be so down now?

Boo:  I would have gotten out today.

## 17

Boo:  You know Tib, kids, dey sure can brighten a household.

Tib:  Dats a nice thing to say Boo, yes dey be gifts from God.

Boo:  No, I mean dey leave de lights on everytime.

## 18

Boo:  Hey Tib, you want a beer?

Tib:  Watts my choices?

Boo:  Yes or No.

## 19

Boo:  Sez here, dat dare be 10000 homeless people in New Orleans.

Tib:  I'd like to help de homeless.

Boo:  So why don't you?

Tib:  They never home.

## 20

Boo:  Me and my little Marie gots into nother bad argument las nite.

Tib:  So who done won the argument?

Boo:  Well she wuz wrong and she forgave me.

## 21

Boo:  I hasn't spoken to de wife now for a week.

Tib:  Are you in nother fight wit her?

Boo:  No, I jus don't likes to interrupt her.

Boo:  Well Tib, here we are on our huntin trip and layin down to sleep. When you looks up, watt you see?

Tib:  Well, I sees thousands and thousands of stars.

23

Boo:  An watt might dat be tellin you my friend.

Tib:  Oh I guess dat dare could be lots of utter planets out dare likes us. And it looks like it's goin to be a nice day to hunt tomorrow. Watt you see?

Boo:  Somebody done stole our tent.

24

Boo:  I sure be enjoyin dis tailgating at de LSU game today but dis beer sure is tasteless and rather pale.

Tib:  Boo, your mug is empty.

25

Boo:  Tib, I had de worstest nightmare las night. I dreamed of these 12 beautiful, fine dancers, blondes, brunettes, redheads, all dancin in a row.

Tib:  Boo, dat don't sounds so bad.

Boo:  Yes it wuz, in my dream, I wuz de third girl from de end.

26

Boo:  Sez here in de paper dey be lookin for a blind man dat done got lost on one dem nudey beaches in Jamica.

Tib:  I wonder how dey goin to find him.

Boo:  Oh, I bet it won't be hard.


27

Boo:  Tib, say you gots a choice, wisdom or all de money you need, watt you choose?

Tib:  I'd take de wisdom.

Boo:  Ok, say you got de wisdom now, watt you got to say now?

Tib:  I should have taken de money.


28

Tib:  Why you and Marie stop havin kids at three?

Boo:  Cuz we heard one out of four kids today is Chinese.


29

Boo:  Watt do you tink fat means Tib?

Tib:  Big I guess.

Boo:  Den watt does slim mean?

Tib:  I guess de opposite, small or skinny.

Boo:  Den how come fat chance and slim chance mean de same ting?

## 30

Boo:  Doctor sez I'm goin to live to be a hundred.

Tib:  Well I'm goin to live forever.

Boo:  Dats so?

Tib:  Dats right. Forever or die tryin.

## 31

Boo:  You know Tib dare be three kinds of people in dis world.

Tib:  Dats so. Watt kind dey are?

Boo:  Dose who can count and dose who can't.

## 32

Boo:  Well you see Tib, big Emma she comes first. Den I come. Den two asses dey come together den I come agin. De two asses come together agin. I den come agin and den pee twice. Den after all dat I come agin.

Old woman:  Young man! Y'all should be ashamed of yourselves talkin such trashy talk.

Tib:  Maam watt you talkin bout? My friend here be teackin me how to spell Mississippi dats all.

Boo:  Sure is a great nite for fishin my friend.

Tib:  Yep it is, jus look at dat full moon.

Boo:  Which you tink be farther away Tib, de moon or lets say Florida.

Tib:  Boo you kiddin me no? Do you tink you can you see Florida from here?

Tib:  Hey I see dat sign in your yard sayin boat for sale but I don't see no boat?

Boo:  I don't gots no boat for sale, can't you see dat ol lawnmower and dat ol bicycle dare by de sign?

Tib:  Yeah, I sees dem dare.

Boo:  So, watt matter wit you den, dey boat for sale.

Tib:  Aw Boo, watt happin, how you got dat big knot on your head?

Boo:  De wife Marie found dis piece paper in my pants dat got de name "Mary Lou" on it.

Tib:  Oh she hit you on head cuz of dat?

Boo:  No, I told her dat wuz de horse I wuz goin to bet on at Evangeline downs today.

Tib:  Den how you gets dat big lump on your head.

Boo: Cuz de horse called for me dis mornin.


## 36

Boo: Man, dat Tanksgivin dinner show wuz fine! I gots to get on some kind of diet fore I get fat.

Tib: Fatter!

Boo: Ha, funny man you are. I'm stuffed. I couldn't eat a nutter bite.

Tib: I'm goin gets some pecan pie, how bout you?

Boo: Sure. But dats it.

Tib: Ice cream wit it?

Boo: Of course.


## 37

Boo: Dem pilgrims show did start a nice tradition wit dis Tanksgivin an all.

Tib: Wonder watt dey be most famous for if dey were alive today?

Boo: Oh I would be guessin dare age.


## 38

Boo: Man I saw dis horse git hit rite in the ass by a truck yesterday.

Tib: Hey don't say ass, say rectum.

Boo:  Rectum? Rectum hell, it killed him.


### 39

Boo:  De family las nit we played dat Trivia Persuit but it ended when I got mad at dem all.

Tib:  Watt happened?

Boo:  Well it be my turn and I got axed, "If you be in a vacuum and someone be callin your name, can you hear em?". I said dats a trick question, dey all sed no, so I got mad and done quit.

Tib:  Why would dat be a trick question?

Boo:  Well you know de answer depends if it be on or off.


### 40

Boo:  I watched one dem biographies las night. Dis one wuz bout dat fighter Mike Tyson.

Tib:  I member him, he wuz some kind of fighter.

Boo:  He sed dat he cries when he has sex.

Tib:  Mace will do dat to you.


### 41

Boo:  Someting must be wrong wit my eyes, I been seein spots all day.

Tib:  Have ever seen a doctor?

Boo:  Nope, just spots.

Boo:  Had to git my truck towed to de service station today, it wouldn't start for me.

Tib:  Watt dey do to gets it runnin agin?

Boo:  Just crap in de carburetor.

Tib:  Aw man, how often you got to do dat now?

Boo:  Sez here dat dey done arrested a transvestite las nite at Fred's bar. Watt in de worl is dis transvestite Tib?

Tib:  Dats someone dat likes to eat, drink, and be Mary.

Boo:  Hey Tib, watt you call 120 white men chasin 1 black man.

Tib:  I don't know, watt?

Boo:  de PGA.

Tib:  Ha funny, man dat Tiger Woods in sum kind of trouble no.

Boo:  You know de difference between a car and a golf ball?

Tib:  Ok, watt?

Boo:  Tiger can drive a golf ball over 300 yards.

## 45

Boo:  I gots a new nick name for dat Tiger Woods.

Tib:  Watts dat?

Boo:  Lion Cheetah.

Tib:  Ha, bet his wife wishes she really wuz a golf widow now.

Boo:  Jus why would Tiger Woods and his wife be out at 3 clock in de morning?

Tib:  "clubbin".

## 46

Boo:  I guess dat Tiger Woods been doin some overtime workin on his schwing.

Tib:  Ha, I'm guessin he can add major screw up to his list of majors.

Boo:  Poor guy got his face all cut up las Friday.

Tib:  Of course, you know dat he always makes his cuts on Friday.

Boo:  I guessin he really is a "scratch" golfer.

## 47

Boo:  I hear dat Obama changed his mind bout sendin dose 35000 troops to dat war.

Tib:  Really, watt he goin to do instead.

Boo:  Send Elin Woods.

Tib: Dat Tiger sure made some news wit hittin a fire hydrant and a tree.

Boo: You know dat makes him just a mailbox and telephone pole short of de grand slam.

## 48

Boo: So Tiger pulled out of dat tournament dis weekend.

Tib: Actually, I tink he done got disqualified.

Boo: DQ'd? For watt?

Tib: Playin de wrong hole.

Boo: Well yous haf to hand it to him, he never wuz lyin to his wife when he would tell her he wuz goin to play a round, ha.

## 49

Boo: Looky here Tib, I done found a 4 leaf clover.

Tib: Lucky you.

Boo: I 'm goin take it home and iron it so it stay flat.

Tib: Don't be pressin your luck.

## 50

Boo: Tib, I needs to take my youngest one's temperature. I finds these thermometers, one be oral and one be rectal. I don't see no difference. Do you knows de difference?

Tib: The taste.

51

Boo: Your mamaw still doin great she is. How old she be now?

Tib: She be goin on 90 now.

Boo: Amazin. And she still don't need no glasses.

Tib: Nope. Drinks straight from de bottle.


52

Boo: Tib, I needs to send dis fax, you know how to do it?

Tib: Oh it be no big deal, just use de one at your job at de plant.

Boo: Yes, I wuz goin to do dat but where does de stamp go on it?


53

Boo: I been readin here in dis Popular Science magazine bout atoms and molecules. Did you know dat photons have mass?

Tib: No, I didn't even know dey were Catholic.


54

Boo: Well we wents to de movies las nite and my Marie, she don'ts like sex in de movies.

Tib: It be offensive to her?

Boo:  Dats rite, de seat kept foldin up on us.


### 55

Boo:  Poor Mrs Sally down de bayou. Yesterday she came to me all upset. She had left home for de store and den her car broke down. She walked all de way back home to find her Pierre and git help. Well she found em in bed wit de teenage girl from next door. She den come over here all cryin and axes me watt to do.

Tib:  Watt you tell her?

Boo:  First I sez check your gas tank and den I sez for her to check de oil.


### 56

Tib:  You know dat it's Christmas time. It bees a time for giving.

Boo:  Dats rite my friend.

Tib:  We should all member dat and give generously.

Boo:  I do accept checks but I prefer de cash.


### 57

Boo:  You know I used to love to watch golf on TV but de doc says I needs to git more exercise.

Tib:  So watt do you doin differant?

Boo:  I watchin tennis.

## 58

Boo:  You know I had one dem endoscopys yesterday. Been tryin to tink of joke there but haven't had any luck.

Tib:  I bet dey be a bit hard to swallow no.

Boo:  Dey be plenty of dem utter end colonoscopy jokes.

Tib:  Yeah but you don't want to make an ass of yoursef.


## 59

Boo:  Look here Tib in dis aquarium, see hows de little bubble be chasin dat big one there, dats a male bubble chasin a female bubble.

Tib:  Is dat so. Den why you tinks he chasin her?

Boo:  To see her bust.


## 60

Boo:  Somebody goin to New Awlens dis weekend axes me today which is fastest way dare.

Tib:  Wuz he walkin or drivin?

Boo:  He wuz drivin.

Tib:  Well dat be de quickest way.


## 61

Boo:  Man I can't waits for de Saints game tomorrow nite.

Tib: You know I'm goin? Den I'm stayin at dat Royal Sonesta Hotel in de quarter after celebratin our win.

Boo: Well lucky you. Hey I stayed at dat place before. Dare towels are way too tick.

Tib: Too tick?

Boo: Dats rite, could hardly close my suitcase when we left.

### 62

Tib: Well Boo, I'm headin to New Orleans to de Saints game.

Boo: You be careful drivin down dare, don't gets lost in one dem bad projects.

Tib: Oh no, I be stayin away from dem places.

Boo: Yep dey bad. I hear Yahoo won't even deliver email dare.

### 63

Tib: Man I had de worse sausage poboy at Fred's las night.

Boo: De sausage wuz dat bad?

Tib: Dats rite. I takes dis big bite out one end of de sausage and I gets a mouth full of corn meal.

Boo: Well Tib, sometimes its hard to make both ends meat.

### 64

Boo: Marie and me went to dat Super Walmart in Breaux Bridge las nite. I lost Marie in dare for bout an hour.

Tib: How you found her den?

Boo:  Well after bout an hour of searchin, I gave up.

Tib:  Den how she found you?

Boo:  Oh, just started talkin to de nearest pretty woman den dare Marie wuz.


## 65

Boo:  Man I'm shore enjoyin dis beer an fishin on dis bayou. Awe man, watt just splattered on my head?

Tib:  Oh Boo, dat crane dat just flew over done pooped on your head.

Boo:  Man I wish I had some toilet paper.

Tib:  Toilet paper? Dat crane must be a 1/2 mile from here by now.


## 66

Boo:  Nice Christmas decorations you got dare

Tib.  Santa and his reindeer. You made dem?

Tib:  Tanks, yep, it took a long time to make dem, paint dem.

Boo:  Why does Rudolf dare have red nose and the utter reindeer behind him dey got brown noses.

Tib:  Cuz dey can't stop as quickly as Rudolf.


## 67

Boo:  You know dare are three stages of our life?

Tib: Really, watt dey are?

Boo: Well stage 1 is when you believes in Santa. Stage 2 is when you don't believes in him no more. Den stage 3 is when you are Santa Claus.

## 68

Tib: Merry Christmas to you too my friend. Your kids seem to be enjoyin it.

Boo: Oh dey are but you know, it just seems like nother day workin at de plant today.

Tib: Like work? Watt you mean?

Boo: Well I did all de work and de man in the suit gets all de credit.

## 69

Boo: So you like de birtday present I gots for you?

Tib: Well it's a nice comb but can't you see dat I be bald.

Boo: Sorry Tib but dat's all I could come up wit.

Tib: Well tanks anyway Boo, I will promise you dis, I'll never part wit it.

## 70

Boo: Pretty Christmas tree you got dare Tib.

Tib: Tank you. Father Pierre sed he liked it too.

Boo: Well dey do have a lots in common.

Tib:  Watt? de Christmas tree and de priest?

Boo:  Yep, dey boat got ornamental balls.


## 71

Tib:  Man I hates workin between Christmas and New Years.

Boo:  Me too. Get this. Some atheist done complained to de boss man at de plant dat we gets all these holidays. He says it's not fair to him and de utters like him to have no holidays.

Tib:  Watt your plant manager do?

Boo:  He says dey can have April 1st.


## 72

Boo:  You can see here Tib my oldest boy gots everyting in his room, he gots color TV, phone, computer, DVD, everyting.

Tib:  Man dats nice. When I wuz a boy, my PaPaw would sends me to my room when I wuz in trouble. So how you punish your boy?

Boo:  I sends him to our room.


## 73

Boo:  Can you believe dat terrorist tryin to blow up dat plane durin Christmas.

Tib:  I know, watt an idiot, watt a coward.

Boo:  Good ting I wasn't dare.

Tib:  Dat's so, watt you would have done?

Boo:  I would have kicked de Shiite out of him.


### 74

Boo:  Well last year my new year's resolution wuz to go to gym 3 times a week.

Tib:  Didn't do so good wit dat one no?

Boo:  Nope, so I gots a new resolution for dis new year. Set my goals a bit lower.

Tib:  Watt be dat? Go once a week?

Boo:  Close. To drive past de gym at least once a week.


### 75

Tib:  Happy New Year Boo!

Boo:  Happy New Year to you too Tib!

Tib:  Say for your new year's resolution, you could try de joggin stead of goin to de gym.

Boo:  I tried dat but it didn't work out.

Tib:  Really? Why not?

Boo:  De ice kept fallin out my bourbon and coke glass.


### 76

Tib:  Sez in de paper dat 10 percent of all auto accidents are caused by drunk drivers.

Boo:  Dats scary.

Tib:  Dat is scary. Wat you tink?

Boo:  It means dat 90 percent of the accidents are caused by stone cold sober drivers.


## 77

Boo:  Poor ol Aucoin down de bayou told me he gots only 6 months to live.

Tib:  Oh dats a shame. He so young, still single right?

Boo:  Dats right. I tells him to get married right away.

Tib:  Get married? Why you think it will make him live longer?

Boo:  No but it will seem longer.


## 78

Boo:  So how's your dog since you took em to de vet yesterday?

Tib:  Well, he got de heart worms but de vet said a shot and some pills would do de job. Den he tells me dat he has dis cow in heat and no bull to take care of it. He axes me if I would have sex wit de cow for 200 dollars.

Boo:  No kiddin. So watt you say to dat?

Tib:  I axed him for a few days to come up wit de money.


## 79

Boo:  You know Tib, I figure if we could just get to be a hundred, we would have it made.

Tib: How's dat?

Boo: Cuz I read dat very few people die past de age of a hundred.


## 80

Boo: You tink I be vain Tib?

Tib: Naw, why you ask?

Boo: Well most good lookin people like me are.


## 81

Boo: Did I tell you dat I be writin a book?

Tib: No I didn't know dat, how far you gotten?

Boo: Well I gots de page numbers done. Now I need to just fill de rest in.


## 82

Boo: Dat woman you be talkin and drinkin wit last night in Fred's bar. How old wuz she?

Tib: She told me she be approachin forty.

Boo: From watt direction?


## 83

Boo: Your dog Herpes, he be one good lookin huntin dog dare.

Tib:  Yes, he bes a pretty good dog.

Boo:  I do be wonderin why you named him Herpes?

Tib:  Cuz he won't heel.


## 84

Boo:  Man it's so cold de lawyers are puttin dare hands in dare own pockets.

Tib:  I bet even Britney Spears be wearin underwear today.

Boo:  I tink I'm goin to have to move my outhouse inside.

Tib:  Dis ice cube I been suckin on is gettin bigger.

Boo:  I tink Hell done froze over.

Tib:  Just in time for de Saints to win de Super Bowl too.


## 85

Boo:  My heatin bill came in wit a warning today, it said "Sit down before opening". I had to chop up mawmaw's piano for firewood, and I only got two chords.

Tib:  I finally got my truck to run but my nose won't stop now. I den take my truck to de store dis morning and I gets de mitten from some irate driver. It bees so cold I saw a hijacker holdin up a picture of his thumb.


## 86

Tib:  Man dat Hebert down de bayou got him a nice lookin wife no?

Boo:  He sure does, she been tryin to get pregnant since dey got married 5 years ago.

Tib:  Maybe he should try wearin boxers.

Boo:  Boxers?

Tib:  Dey say wearin dem helps get a woman pregnant.

Boo:  Maybe so but I tink dey have better chance if he didn't wear nuttin at all.


## 87

Boo:  I see dat Mark McQuire wishes he done confessed to steroids earlier now?

Tib:  It's cuz he didn't have de balls to do it back den.

Boo:  Ha, you knows watt steroids and hurricanes have in common?

Tib:  No? Watt's dat?

Boo:  Dey both sure can make dem Jamicans run fast.


## 88

Tib:  I see your prized pig in de yard dare, he only got 3 legs now?

Boo:  Dat's rite. You member how dat pig saved my life last year. A gator done bit down on my foot and started draggin back into de bayou. Dat pig came over and scared him off.

Tib:  Yep, dat pig is a hero. So watt happened to his leg?

Boo:  Hey a pig like dat you don't eat all at once.

## 89

Boo:  You know I tink I done married a nun these days.

Tib:  A nun, why you sey dat?

Boo:  Cuz I gets none in de mornin, I gets none in de evenin, and I don't gets none at all lessin I beg.


## 90

Boo:  Me and Marie done got in nutter fight las night but we ok now.

Tib:  How yall settled it den?

Boo: Well got her to meet me halfway. I admitted I wuz wrong and she admitted she wuz right.


## 91

Boo:  You hear dat Hebert went skydivin las weekend?

Tib:  Hebert is blind, I can't believes it. Did he do ok?

Boo:  Oh he did fine, but it sure scared de heck out of his dog though.


## 92

Tib:  Dey gots dis new "carbon" diet dat be more friendly to de environment.

Boo:  Watt? You kiddin no?

Tib:  No. Its sposed to reduce dis so called green house effect on de atmosphere.

Boo: Dat sounds crazy. Why not just tell everybody to stay away from Taco Bell.

### 93

Boo: My Marie she shows off dis new bra to me last night.

Tib: Really, someting special.

Boo: Oh yes, really nice one, reminded of one dem sheep dogs, I calls it a sheep dog bra.

Tib: Sheep dog bra?

Boo: Yep, it rounded dem up really nice and pointed dem in the right direction.

### 94

Boo: Hey Tib, you gots some pepper out dare.

Tib: Why sure, gots lots of pepper. You want black or white pepper.

Boo: Neither you dummy, I needs toilet pepper.

### 95

Boo: De wife complains dat I makes too much noise when we make love.

Tib: Cuz it might wake up de kids?

Boo: No, cuz it wakes her up.

# 96

Boo: My youngin's teacher called me last night and jumped my ass bout takin him huntin.

Tib: Why? Cuz she tinks he too young?

Boo: No worse, she said dat I be teachin and equipin him to become a violent killer one day.

Tib: You gots to be kiddin me. Watt you say to her?

Boo: I sed "Well you be equipped to be a prostitute den why ain't you one?"

# 97

Tib: So you bet on sum horses dis weekend?

Boo: Naw, I done given up de gamblin.

Tib: You? No way, you won't be able to quit gamblin.

Boo: Oh I bet you I can.

# 98

Tib: Glad you be gamblin agin. I still can't believes your dog here be playin poker wit us.

Boo: Yep, he been playin since he wuz a pup.

Tib: Dat is de smartest dog I ever seen.

Boo: Oh he not dat smart, he always wags his tail when he has a good hand.

Tib:  Hey Boo, why you cryin now.

Boo:  Just tinkin bout Pawpaw and watt his last words were.

Tib:  Your pawpaw passed 5 years go now, watt he say.

Boo:  He sed to member him when he gets de Saints into de super bowl for me.

Tib:  Who dat goin to beat dem Saints!

Boo:  Watt a joke dat so called singles bar we stopped at in Lafayette last night.

Tib:  You right dare. Did you noticed someting in common wit all de men dare too?

Boo:  Yep, dey were all married too.

Tib:  Watt's your Zodiac sign?

Boo:  I be a Sagittarius but I believes none of dat stuff.

Tib:  How come?

Boo:  Us Sagittarius'es be skeptical.

## A little lagniappe 1

Tib:  You still in de dog house wit de wife?

Boo:  Oh yes my friend.

Tib:  You know dare bees two theories on arguing wit de women.

Boo: Tell me dem pleaze.

Tib: Sorry, neither works.

## A little lagniappe 2

Tib:  Watt side of de bed you do sleepin on?

Boo:  I'm on left side of course.

Tib:  Why is dat?

Boo:  Even when my Marie is sleepin, she got to be right.

## A little lagniappe 3

Boo:  Well I be in de dog house agin wit Marie. Can't win.

Tib:  Dat on goin battle of de sexes no?

Boo:  You tink we ever goin to win de battle of de sexes one day?

Tib:  No way. There be way to much fraternizin wit de enemy.

# A little lagniappe 4

Tib: Can you believed de supreme court sez our American money is not fair for blind people.

Boo: Dats crazy. I can tell difference between one dollar bills and de utters witout lookin at em.

Tib: How you do dat?

Boo: By de smell of dem.

Tib: Smell?

Boo: Dats rite. De one dollar bills smell like strippers.


# A little lagniappe 5

Tib: Aw Boo, watt happen to you, your face be covered in blood?

Boo: Well, see dat rake over dare layin in de yard?

Tib: I sees it.

Boo: Well I didn't.


# A little lagniappe 6

Tib: So watt percentage of all de women get into Heaven you tink?

Boo: Oh, I be guessin bout 25, no say tirty percent.

Tib: Only tirty pecent?

Boo: Dat's right, anymore den dat, den it would be Hell.

## 2-1

Tib:  Just wonderin, when you and Mah ree be makin love, does she have her eyes open or closed.

Boo:  Closed of course.

Tib:  Of course? Whys dat?

Boo:  You tink she would dare allow herself to see me passin a good time.

## 2-2

Boo:  Well my little brother going to quit de army for good now.

Tib:  Whys dat?

Boo:  Well he sez it used to be illegal to be gay in de army. Now it be optional.

Tib:  So why he quittin?

Boo:  He got no problem it being optional, he sez he be gettin out before Obama make it mandatory.

## 2-3

Boo:  I read in de Popular Science last night dat NASA spent 12 billion dollars makin a pen dat could write in space no matter de temperature.

Tib:  Dats interestin. Let me axe you someting?

Boo: Watts dat?

Tib: Why didn't dey just use a pencil?


## 2-4

Boo: I wents to see Aunt Lilly at de nursin home today.

Tib: How's she doin?

Boo: Well we goes outside to a bench to visit. As we be talkin, she begins to lean to de left, out of nowheres, a nurse rushes up to her and straightens her out. A little later, she starts to leans to de right and dis doctor rushes up and straightens her up.

Tib: Dats nice.

Boo: Well she sed, "It's nice, but dey don't let you fart."


## 2-5

Tib: I see you gots a nutter black eye dare, Mah ree?

Boo: Dats right. I axes her bout makin love last night.

Tib: So watt happened?

Boo: We were watchin dat millionaire game show. I axes her bout makin love right den. Well she said No. I den axed her if dat was her final answer. She said yes. So den I sed dat I'd like to phone a fren and dats when I got dis black eye.


## 2-6

Boo: Tib I tink you missed de turn here, you need to turn round.

Tib: Ok, makin U turn now, uh oh, I tink dat might be an illegal U turn I just made.

Boo: Oh don't worry, de policeman behind us just did de same ting.



## 2-7

Tib: Careful dare Boo, you just drove true dat red light.

Boo: Dats ok, cousin Prejean does it all de time.

Tib: Ai yi yi, you just ran a nutter red light.

Boo: Dats ok, Prejean does it all de time.

Tib: Ok why you stoppin now, de light is green here?

Boo: Prejean might be coming de utter way.



## 2-8

Tib: So you took your woman out on actual date las night. So how was your date?

Boo: Not so good. Mah ree she slap me tree times.

Tib: Fightin you off no?

Boo: No, to keep me awake.



## 2-9

Boo: Us drivin home from Fred's bar tonight reminds me of my Uncle Bertrand's last word.

Tib: Watt was it?

Boo: Truck!

## 2-10

Boo: Yo ma maw so fat her cereal bowl came wit a lifeguard.

Tib: Yo ma maw so fat her blood type is Ragu.

Boo: Yo ma maw so fat I gots to take tree steps back just to see all of her.

Tib: Yo ma maw so fat you gots to drive a four-wheeler round to git to her good side.

Boo: Yo mama!

## 2-11

Tib: Yo ma maw so fat dat I ran round her twice den got lost.

Boo: Yo ma maw so fat dat no one can talk behind her back.

Tib: Yo ma maw so fat she ain't on a diet, she's on a try it.

Boo: Yo ma maw so fat dat she fell in love and broke it.

Tib: Yo mama!

## 2-12

Boo: Yo ma maw so fat she got to get out de car to change gears.

Tib: Yo ma maw so fat gits her clothes in tree sizes, extra large, jumbo and oh-my-God-it's-comin-at-us!

Boo:  Yo ma maw so fat she keeps dollars in one pocket and pesos in de utter pocket.

Tib:  Yo ma maw so fat her weight and phone number are de same number.

Boo:  Yo mama!


## 2-13

Tib:  Yo ma maw so fat she wakes up in parts.

Boo:  Yo ma maw so fat she got smaller fat women orbitin round her.

Tib:  Yo ma maw so fat dat she's 36-24-36 in her feet.

Boo:  Yo ma maw so fat de elephants throw peanuts at her.

Tib:  Yo mama!


## 2-14

Tib:  Can you believe dat our ma maws are goin to de Superbowl.

Boo:  Yo ma maw so fat dat when she goes to de Superbowl, she sits next to everyone.

Tib:  Yo ma maw so fat dat when she lay on dat Miami beach, dose Greenpeace people try to push her back into de water.

Boo:  Yo ma maw so fat her nickname is "Eclipse".

Tib:  Yo ma maw so fat dat when God sed "Let dare be light" he told her to move her ass out de way.

Boo:  Yo mama!

Boo:  Watt cha call a bunch of millionaires sittin round watchin de SuperBowl?

Tib:  Don't know?

Boo:  de Minnesota Vikings!

Tib:  SAINTS stands for Saints Are I N The Superbowl!

Boo:  Ha, den COLTS means Count On Losin The Superbowl.

Boat:  GEAUX SAINTS!

Boo:  De Saints done won de Superbowl!

Tib:  No joke?

Boo:  No joke.

Boo:  I still cannots believe we done won de Superbowl.

Tib:  Me neither my mah fren, I heard dat a couple of Saints got arrested for exposing demselves down in Miami.

Boo:  Did dey get to keep de beads?

Tib:  Merci Saints!

Tib:  You member bein born?

Boo:  Naw, you gots to member I was born at very early age.

Tib:  I bet since he was a kid, Archie Manning dreamed bout throwing de winning touchdown pass for de Saints in de Superbowl one day.

Boo:  Well at least his son Peyton did.


### 2-19

Boo:  Man watt a great Superbowl no?

Tib:  Yep. And dose commercials, specially de beer commercials, sure have sum good lookin women on it.

Boo:  Dey sure do, but you notice someting missin in dem?

Tib:  No? Watt dat?

Boo:  Not a single man in dose commercials has a beer belly.


### 2-20

Marie:  Whose dat drunk woman over dare you keeps starin at.

Boo:  You member her, she wuz my ol girlfriend before you. She took to de drinkin after we broke up and I hear dat hasn't been sober since.

Marie:  My lord, who would have taught she would be celebratin dat long.


### 2-21

Boo:  I gots a ticket today from Sheriff Blanchard for not stoppin completely at a stop sign.

Tib:  Slow down, stop, same ting no?

Boo:  Dat's watt I said. Watts de difference I axes.

Tib:  So dats why you got dose lumps on your head now?

Boo:  He started hittin me on de head wit his baton den axes if I want him to stop or slow down. Watts de difference?


## 2-22

Boo:  I dreamed las night dat Dolly Parton wuz my momma.

Tib:  Hey dat not bad no?

Boo:  It is if de dream has me as a bottle baby.


## 2-23

Boo:  Las night, my Mah ree wuz drivin us home when all sudden de truck broke down.

Tib:  Puncture?

Boo:  No but I sure wanted to.


## 2-24

Tib:  Aw Boo, why you got two black eyes.

Boo:  From work at de plant. Saw dis woman standin dare with her skirt stuck in her butt crack. I pulls it out for her den she turns and punches me in de eye.

Tib:  So how you got the 2nd black eye.

Boo:  I taught she liked it dat way so I tried to push it back in.


## 2-25

Tib:  Sez here in de paper dat insanity is heredity.

Boo:  Oh I believes dat, you gits it from your children.

Tib:  Talks bout cloning too, how dey got to makes all kinds of new laws for dem.

Boo:  Hey, clones are people two.


## 2-26

Boo:  Man my stomach bees upset today.

Tib:  You know four out of five people suffer from diarrhea.

Boo:  Does dat mean dat one in five enjoys it?

Tib:  Dey say it might be hereditary.

Boo:  I believes dat. It runs in your jeans.

Tib:  On de utter hand, dares always constipation to steal your time.

Boo:  True, but diarrhea waits for no man.


## 2-27

Boo:  I had de full blown stereo system blarin in my truck today.

Tib:  Is dat so?

Boo:  Dats right. Had de wife in front and her momma in back.


## 2-28

Boo:  Mah ree's sister is all worried bout bein an old maid. Worried bout findin a husband.

Tib:  Watt wise words of wisdom you gave her mah fren.

Boo:  I told her she needs to stop lookin for a husband, start lookin for a bachelor.


## 2-29

Tib:  Watts dat big hole you diggin dare?

Boo:  It's for my youngest girl's pet goldfish.

Tib:  Goldfish? Dats a big hole for a goldfish.

Boo:  Oh not really, it's inside de neighbor's cat.


## 2-30

Tib:  Ol Mrs Theriot done past away today. Less den a month after her husband past.

Boo:  Second husband you know. She had ten kids wit de first and eight wit de second one.

Tib:  Well tank God de two of dem are together at last.

Boo:  You talkin bout her first or second husband.

Tib:  Neither, I'm talkin bout her legs.

Boo:  Man it was nice de Saints won de Superbowl but I hopes dey don't win it agin nex year.

Tib:  Why not?

Boo:  Cuz I'm tired of dis cold weather.

Boo:  Well I done fell off de Lent last night.

Tib:  Oh no, watt happened?

Boo:  You know we gives up de sex for lent and it's been many weeks now since de Lent started. Well las night, I sees my Mah ree leaning over de freezer and I couldn't hep myself, I plugged her rite den and dare.

Tib:  Aw Boo! You better be careful, you could get thrown out de church for dat.

Boo:  It gits you thrown out of de Winn Dixie too.

Boo:  Ifin I die first, would you say sum nice words at de grave for me?

Tib:  Sure mah fren, and for me if I go first, would you pour a bottle of my favorite Crown over my grave.

Boo:  No problem wit dat. No problem at tall. But one more ting, you mind if it passes through my kidneys first?

Boo:  I reads here in de Picayune dat dey did a survey in New Awlens bout all de Mexicans dare since Katrina. Dey axed if de people dare taught it was a problem.

Tib:  Watt de survey say?

Boo:  Well it sez dat 30 percent sed it was a big problem. De rest sed "No es una problema seriosa."

Boo:  Hey Tib, de wife wants me to pull de weeds from her little garden here but all de plants look de same to me. How am I supposed to knows de difference.

Tib:  Dats easy, when you pulls de plant out de ground and it comes up easy, it's one of de good plants.

Tib:  I see here in de paper nutter one dem movie stars goin into rehab.

Boo:  Rehab! Rehab is for quitters.

Boo:  You know Tib, I feel sorry for dem people dat don't drink.

Tib:  Me too. Too bad dey can't be enjoyin dis beer like us. So why you feel sorry for dem?

Boo: Cuz when dey wakes up in de morning, dats as good as dey goin to feel all day.

## 2-38

Boo: Well de plant manager axes me if I believes in life after death today.

Tib: Why he axes you dat?

Boo: Member yesterday, I took off to go fishin wit you. I told de plant manager dat I had to go to papaw's funeral.

Tib: Ok, so?

Boo: Well papaw stopped by to see me yesterday.

## 2-39

Boo: Dares dis study dat sez dat breast-feedin can boost your IQ, make you smarter.

Tib: Ha I'm guessin you're tryin it.

Boo: Yep but it justs makes my nipples sore.

## 2-40

Boo: You know while we were drinkin last night sum burglar broke into my house.

Tib: Oh no Boo. Did he gits anyting?

Boo: Oh just broken jaw, bunch of teeth knocked out and couple of broken ribs.

Tib: Your Mah ree did dat?

Boo: Sure did. She taught it wuz me comin home drunk.

## 2-41

Tib: You know St Patrick's day coming up no? You know why dey celebrate St Patrick's day?

Boo: Irish I knew.

Tib: It's celebrates St Patrick who drove de snakes out of Ireland.

Boo: Oh I know dat, I know why he drove dem out.

Tib: Whys dat?

Boo: Cuz too expensive to fly dem out..

## 2-42

Boo: De sheriff stops me last night when I wuz walkin home from Fred's bar.

Tib: Watt he do?

Boo: He axes me where I wuz goin. I sed I was headin for a lecture.

Tib: Lecture, who be given a lecture at 2 in de mornin?

Boo: De wife.

## 2-43

Tib: I see you gots a new dog? Dats sum big pit bull you gots dare. Watt yall name him?

Boo: I came up wit de name "Egypt".

Tib: Eygpt? Dats different. So why dat name?

Boo: Cuz he be leavin little pyramids everywhere.


## 2-44

Boo: See how all de utter dogs out dare sit down when my dog Egypt walks by.

Tib: I see. Dey must respect him no?

Boo: Don't tink so. It's cuz he has a very cold nose.


## 2-45

Boo: You know I tink I gots de smartest dog in Louisiana.

Tib: Don't tink so. I gots de smartest dog.

Boo: Oh yeah. Well mine runs down street and buys me paper every mornin and brings it to me.

Tib: I know dat.

Boo: How you know dat?

Tib: My dog told me.


## 2-46

Boo: I gettin kind of sick of de new dog Egypt. He always be chasin people on a bike.

Tib: You tink you goin to have to give him away or put him down?

Boo:  Awe no. I tink I'm just goin to take de bike away.


### 2-47

Boo:  Who wuz dat nice lookin women I saw you wit at Fred's bar las night?

Tib:  Oh someone from school.

Boo:  Teacher?

Tib:  Nope, didn't have to.


### 2-48

Tib:  You know, Mah ree is one pretty woman you got dare Boo. I bet you tinks twice before leavin her alone at night.

Boo:  Right you are. First, I have to tink up reason for goin out. Second, I have to tink of reason why she can't come.


### 2-49

Boo:  Look at Aucoin over dare fishin down de bayou from us.

Tib:  I see him. De man likes to drink no. I tink he be one dem alcoholics.

Boo:  I bet you're right. He wuz at Fred's bar drinkin next to us all night las night.


### 2-50

Boo:  I done forgot, when's your birtday Tib?

Tib:  March 22th.

Boo:  Which year?

Tib:  Every year.

## 2-51

Boo:  Can you believe dat Nancy Pelosi. She sum kind of crooked politician no?

Tib:  All dem politicians are crooked, dey all like diapers.

Boo:  Diapers?

Tib:  Dats right. Dey should be changed often, and for de same reason.

## 2-52

Tib:  Hey dare my sheree. Let me buy you a few drinks to loosen you up.

Missy:  No you're not!

Tib:  Come on sheree. I'm goin to take you home now.

Missy:  Oh no you're not!

Tib:  I'm goin to make love to you all nite long.

Missy:  Oh no you're not!

Tib:  And I ain't goin to use no protection neither.

Missy:  Oh yes you are!

## 2-53

Boo:  Man dis given up de sex for de Lent has been tough.

Tib:  It hasn't been easy for me neither given up alcohol.

Boo:  I gave up alcohol last year for de Lent.

Tib:  You did? Don't member dat?

Boo:  Wuz de longest 20 minutes of my life.


## 2-54

Boo:  Man de wife and I had one dem fancy bottles of wine last night. The kind wit de cork. Wuz sum good.

Tib:  Well dey say wine improves wit age.

Boo:  Oh you gots dat right. De older I get de better I like it.


## 2-55

Tib:  Boo, you ever tried sniffin coke.

Boo:  Coke? I tried sniffin coke one time long time go.

Tib:  You did?

Boo:  Yes but de ice cubes kept getting stuck in my nose.


## 2-56

Tib:  How many seconds you tink dey are in a year?

Boo:  Twelve. De second of January, de second of February, and so on.

## 2-57

Boo: Man I love listenin to dat Dolly Parton on de radio.

Tib: Me too. I heard she wuz a school teacher once.

Boo: Teacher? I don't tink so?

Tib: Whys dat?

Boo: Well every time she turned round she would be wiping de blackboard clean.

## 2-58

Boo: You realize dat dare are 24 beers in a case and 24 hours in a day.

Tib: Coincidence?

Boo: Oh I tink not.

Tib: You tinks we drinks to excess?

Boo: No, I tinks we drinks to anyting.

## 2-59

Boo: You had any luck down at Fred's bar las night?

Tib: Well I did meet dis one, she had beautiful long curly black hair dat fell down her back.

Boo: Hmmm, interestin no?

Tib: I just wish she had it on her head too.

Boo:  Last night I decided to cut through Benoits cow pasture on my walk back from Fred's bar but it took me hour longer to git home.

Tib:  Whys dat?

Boo:  Well I gets halfway across dare and den I loses my hat.

Tib:  You couldn't find it?

Boo:  Worse. I must of tried on at least 50 utter "hats" before I finally found mine.

Boo:  My youngest boy be learnin de fiddle lately at de house. Problem is dat everyting he plays makes de dogs howl sum fierce.

Tib:  Den tell em to play a song de dogs don't know.

Boo:  You seen dat new bar down de bayou yet?

Tib:  You mean de Prop Stop, been dare.

Boo:  Yes dats it. Dey serve women dare?

Tib:  I wish.  You gots to bring your own.

Boo:  Hey Tib, you gots any of dem geraniums growings in your flower garden dare?

Tib: No sir, but I gots sum pretty African violets if you wants sum?

Boo: No dat won't do, it was de geraniums dat Mah ree axed me to water while she been gone.

## 2-64

Boo: It sez here dat de average American car now weighs 500 pounds more den it was 10 years ago.

Tib: Dey must be countin de average American is sittin in it too.

## 2-65

Boo: Here's your beer Tib.

Tib: Tanks. Oh dare's a fly in my mug. I got it out here. Oh you gots one in your mug too Boo.

Boo: I do? I see it. Come here you little brat. Now you spit it dat beer back in de mug you little thief.

## 2-66

Tib: I been to de health club tree times this week. I'm be sure sore.

Boo: I joined dat club too you know, cost me $400 dollars.

Tib: So how is it goin den?

Boo: Well I haven't lost a pound. It seems dat you have to go dare too.

2-67

Boo: Been readin bout de Middle East. I figure dem Jewish people dat live dare can't stand Moses.

Tib: Moses? He freed all de jews, how can dat be?

Boo: Well look how dey travelled 40 years on de desert and dey end up settlin in de only place dat gots no oil.


2-68

Boo: Hey Tib, fancy seein you here at de casino.

Tib: Hey Boo, wonder why de power went out.

Boo: I don't know but I'm stuck on dis escalator since it went out.

Tib: Why don't you just walk down?

Boo: I can't, I wuz goin up.


2-69

Boo: I heard Mah ree given our oldest daughter sum advice las night.

Tib: Good no?

Boo: Well sort of, she said "Cook a man a fish, you feed him for a day..."

Tib: I know dat one, "Teach him to fish, you can feed em for a lifetime" right?

Boo: No, she said "Teach him to fish, you can get rid of him for de whole weekend".

2-70

Boo:  De plant manager accused me of goin to golfin yesterday wit you when I called in sick.

Tib:  Uh oh. Watt you say to dat?

Boo:  I told him he wuz wrong and we had de fish to prove it.


2-71

Boo:  De plant manager got on my case agin today when I got to work a little bit late.

Tib:  Watt you say?

Boo:  I told him dat I had overslept but he didn't like dat excuse.

Tib:  Watt he say?

Boo:  He scoffed at me and sed he was surprised to hear dat I needed to sleep at home too.


2-72

Boo:  Let me axe you sum word questions from de youngest homework las night.

Tib:  Okay, go ahead an axe me someting.

Boo:  Use de word "information" in a sentence.

Tib:  Ducks sometimes fly information.

Boo:  Watt does benign mean.

Tib:  Benign is watt you be after you be eight.

Boo: Here's sum more questions from de youngest homework.

Tib: Okay, I'm ready.

Boo: Use de word "fascinate" in a sentence.

Tib: Hmm, Dis shirt has nine buttons but I can only fascinate.

Boo: Watt does "varicose" mean.

Tib: Nearby

Boo: Okay, las one, where was de "Magna Carter" signed.

Tib: At de bottom.

Boo: If you were to give your wife an Indian name, watt you would name her?

Tib: Hmmm, let me see, I guess I would go wit "Broken Wind".

Boo: Ha good one. I would give my dear Mah ree de name "Five Horses".

Tib: Dats strange, why dat one?

Boo: Nag, nag, nag, nag, nag.

Boo: I hear sum more of your in-law's folks followin sum of dare own up to Missiouri, goin to live dare too.

Tib:  Dats right, good riddance too.

Boo:  Wonder why so many of dat family movin dare.

Tib:  You know watt dey say, "Missouri loves company."


### 2-76

Tib:  You heard dat sum guy on a motorcycle ran into a woman yesterday.

Boo:  Really, why was he ridin in de kitchen?


### 2-77

Boo:  Watt does de last 4 letters in American say.

Tib:  I CAN.

Boo:  Watt does de last 4 letters in Republican say.

Tib:  I CAN.

Boo:  Watt does de last 4 letters in Democrats say.

Tib:  RATS.

Boo:  Dats all I'm sayin.


### 2-78

Boo:  Heard dat crazy Gaudet wuz caught agin flashin people dat motor by his camp. I taught he done retired from doin dat.

Tib:  I heard he's goin to stick out for anutter year.

## 2-79

Boo:  Watt does bigamy mean Tib?

Tib:  Dats one wife too many.

Boo:  Hmmm, den watt does monogamy mean?

Tib:  Same ting.

## 2-80

Boo:  Did you hear dat crazy Gaudet flashed three old women sittin on a bench at Girald park yesterday?

Tib:  Really?

Boo:  Two of de women had a stroke.

Tib:  I guess de utter one couldn't reach?

## 2-81

Boo:  Dat was sum heavy woman I saw you talkin to at Fred's las night.

Tib:  Hey dats not nice. I wouldn't say dat bout her, but when she bent over I did see her G-rope.

## 2-82

Boo:  My attempts at given sum discipline to de oldest daughter for comin in too late las night didn't work out no good.

Tib:  Really?

Boo: Lets just say you should never ever raise a hand to your children.

Tib: Whys dat?

Boo: It leaves de groin unprotected.

## 2-83

Tib: De Cormiers down de bayou, dey been tryin to have a baby wit no luck. Well dey gets a call today dat dares a Russian baby boy ready for dem to come and adopt.

Boo: Well good for dem. I'm happy for dem. I guess dey better sign up at LSU for one dem night courses to learn sum Russian no?

Tib: For when dey travel to git him?

Boo: No no, so dat dey know watt dat new baby be sayin when he starts to talkin.

## 2-84

Boo: Let me axes you a question from de youngest homework here. Ok, give me a sentence dat starts wit "I".

Tib: Okay, "I is..."

Boo: Whoa dare, you means "I am" no?

Tib: Okay, "I am de ninth letter in de alphabet."

## 2-85

Boo: I tried to sign on to de bank online yesterday but I kept seein dees stars when I typed de password.

Tib: Oh dats is so no one can see your password when someone is standin behind you.

Boo: Is dat so? Well dey still showed up agin today when no one was behind me.

## 2-86

Boo: Young Miss Savoie came an tole me bout her new little one and how she can't sleep at night worryin bout not hearin de baby in de nex room ifin de baby were to fall out it's crib.

Tib: I'm sure you gave her sum good advice no.

Boo: Yep. Told her to take de carpet out de room.

## 2-87

Boo: I offered to help my oldest girl wit her history paper las night. She axes me to use de internet and do sum research for her.

Tib: Did you have any luck?

Boo: Oh yes. I found at least 10 people dat sell dem.

## 2-88

Boo: Daughter grounded for comin in too late las night. She went on and on bout how she been wit dozens of boys and she hasn't let one of dem kiss her.

Tib: Well dats good no?

Boo: No exactly. She said de one was a boy name Jimmy.

Boo:  Man I'm sum tired. Aucoin down de bayou got a mule wit such long ears dat when it hits de door, dat makes it kick someting fearse. So I spent de whole yesterday helpin Aucoin raise dat barn so it's ears don't hit de door.

Tib:  Why you didn't just dig out de doorway, makin it deeper.

Boo:  Tib you sum kind of idiot no.  It wuz de mule's ears dat wuz too long, not de legs.

## 2-90

Boo:  Okay, tells me watt you tink of dis paintin of de bayou I did last night.

Tib:  Well I tink it be worthless.

Boo:  Dat's okay, I still want to hear it anyway.

## 2-91

Boo:  Went to de dentist today and he pulled my aching tooth, costs me $85 dollars.

Tib:  85 dollars! Dats a lot for a few minutes of work no?

Boo:  Dats watt I sed. But den he sed he could could make it last all day long if I wanted too.

Tib:  I wonder if your dentist has anything for yellow teeth.

Boo:  A brown tie.

Boo:  My sister-in-the-law and her husband done axes me to help name dare just born twins. Dey had a boy and girl. I suggested Denise for de girl but couldn't tink of one for de boy. You got any ideas?

Tib:  De nephew.

Boo: Ok, my Mah ree axes me to dig dis hole to plants a tree yesterday. After I dug it she changes her mind and says she wants to put it on utter side of yard. So I goes to put de dirt back in but I couldn't get all de dirt back in dare. I had to leaves a little pile on top of it. I wonder why dat is?

Tib: Dats easy, it's cuz you didn't dig de hole deep enough in de first place.

Tib:  Hey Boo, can I borrow a hundred dollars from you?

Boo:  Now Tib, you know I don't likes loanin money to mah frens.

Tib:  Ok, can I borrow a hundred dollars feet pue tan (you son of b*tch)?

Boo:  My truck done broke down, can you give me a lift Tib?

Tib:  Why sure, "You look good for your age mah fren".

Tib:  So watts your plans for Mother's day Boo?

Boo:  Take mom out to dinner den take Mah ree out somewheres tonight I guess.

Tib:  Dat Mah ree sum good mom no?

Boo: I tink so. In fact she would be de perfect mother if she weren't so busy raisin de kids.

Tib:  Man Boo, you played sum great golf today, I don't tink you hit one bad shot. And your dog, I liked how he would stand up on it's back legs and clap for you.

Boo:  Yep, he does dat each time I have good shot.

Tib:  Watt he do when you have bad shot.

Boo:  Oh does three or four flips in de air. Depends on how hard I kick him.

Tib:  So how de oldest daughter do in de swim meet today?

Boo:  She came in last in de 100 meter breaststroke. She claims de utter girls cheated.

Tib:  Cheated, how?

Boo:  She sed dat the utter girls used dare hands.

Tib: I member my dad taught me how to swim by throwing me out in middle of bayou and makin me swim back.

Boo: Me too.

Tib: Swimmin through de snakes and gators wuz toughest part.

Boo: For me it wuz gettin out of de bag.

2-100

Tib: Supposin you were goin to die of cancer and only had tree months to get your affairs in order, watt you would do?

Boo: Well first ting I'd be doin is tellin everyone I was dyin of AIDS.

Tib: A IDS? But you dyin of cancer, why you tell everyone AIDS?

Boo: S o dat you and my utter frens I got wouldn't be goin after my Mah ree after I'm gone.

Tib: Ha, dats watt I call gettin your affairs in order.

2-101

Boo: Man, you sum stupid in dis dream I had las night.

Tib: Watt I do dis time?

Boo: We wuz stranded out in de gulf on dis boat wit nuttin but dis lamp. I rubbed de lamp and dis genie comes out of it. He grants us one wish and before I could say anyting, you said to turn de gulf into beer.

Tib:  Beer, dat sounds like a good ting no?

Boo:  It wuz but den it meant we had to pee in de boat after dat.

## A little lagniappe 1

Boo:  So how wuz dat pretty little one I saw you wit las night at Fred's.

Tib:  Oh she wuz nice for couple hours, den de naggin started.

Boo:  Really dat quick.

Tib:  Yeah, first it wuz "I wanna know your name" den it wuz...


## A little lagniappe 2

Tib:  Dats an interestin golf ball you got dare.

Boo:  It sure is, it's de latest ting in golf. If you go into de bushes, it beeps. If it goes in water, it floats. If it gets dark, it lights up.

Tib:  Wow, watt a ball. Where you git it?

Boo:  I found it in de woods over dare.


## A little lagniappe 3

Tib:  Dat garden you got growin dare sure is lookin great.

Boo:  Tank you Tib, it wuz hard work.

Tib:  Amazin watt you can do wit a little help from God.

Boo:  Dats true, but you should have seen how it looked when God had it all by himself.

## A little lagniappe 4

Tib:  Dats a nice job you did wit your new mail box dare.

Boo:  Tanks, dat paintin wuz hardest part.

Tib:  Nice letterin you did but you spelled mail "m a l e".

Boo:  Dats wrong?

Tib:  You know you sposed to start it wit capital M.

## A little lagniappe 5

Tib: S o your oldest boy bout to graduate from high school. Watts he want to do next.

Boo:  He wants to be a garbage man.

Tib:  A garbage man? Whys dat?

Boo:  Dats right. Cuz he tinks dey only work 2 days a week.

## A little lagniappe 6

Boo:  De youngest been pesterin me forever to take her to de zoo. So yesterday I took her but Mah rees all upset wit me now.

Tib: Why she be upset bout you takin de little one to de zoo.

Boo: Well it started when de youngster told Mah ree how excited I got when one of de animals came in at 20 to 1.

Boo: Man dis diet dat my Mah ree gots me on is killin me and it's been only one day.

Tib: Don't worry mah fren, de second day is always easier.

Boo: Is dat so?

Tib: Cuz you'll be off it by den.

## 3-1

Boo:  Here you go Tib, nice juicy steak right off de pit my friend.

Tib:  I noticed dat you were pressin it to de plate wit your thumb.  Dat's kind of uncleanly no?

Boo:  Well, it would be more uncleanly if I drop it agin.

## 3-2

Tib:  So how wuz your niece's wedding yesterday?

Boo:  Oh it wuz nice but de food? It wuz great.

Tib:  Watt dey have to eat?

Boo:  I have a record of everyting I ate dare.  Let me go get my tie.

## 3-3

Boo:  Tib, how wuz de wife's Geaux family reunion?

Tib:  Oh I past a good time dare, saw lots of our ol friends dare.

Boo:  I member dat good lookin but dizzy aunt dey had, watts her name?

Tib:  Oh, dat be Verty Geaux.

Boo:  Did you see dat uncle who always had de constipation trouble at de Geaux reunion?

Tib: You mus be talkin bout Cant Geaux.

## 3-4

Boo: Did dat cousin dat lives in Illinois come to de Geaux family reunion?

Tib: Yep, Chica Geaux wuz dare.

Boo: How bout de cousin dat lives down in Mexico now, wuz she at de reunion?

Tib: I tinks so, I tink I saw Amy Geaux dare.

Boo: How bout her brother dat lives on de border dare.

Tib: Oh yes, Green Geaux wuz dare.

## 3-5

Boo: How bout de aunt dats a dance teacher, wuz she at de Geaux family reunion.

Tib: Tang Geaux wuz dare.

Boo: Her sister dat does dancing at de Gold club.

Tib: Go Geaux showed up too.

Boo: Wuz de great great grand pa at de reunion, de one worked on de stage coaches?

Tib: Wellsfar wuz dare. He still around.

3-6

Boo:  Did dat cousin dat travels all over de states come to de Geaux family reunion. Watt her name wuz?

Tib:  Winnie Bay Geaux did stop by.  She had dat crazy jumpy son of hers dare too.

Boo:  Oh yes, Poe Geaux.  How bout dat fruit lovin cousin from Florida, wuz he dare?

Tib:  I tink I member seein Mang Geaux dare.

Boo:  Oh, dat boy from Ellis U, de one dat teaches positive tinkin dare?

Tib:  Yep, Wayto made it too.


3-7

Boo:  Did cousin dat works de convenience store in town come to de Geaux reunion?

Tib:  Yep, Stopn Geaux wuz dare.

Boo:  How bout de magician one?

Tib:  I tink so, I saw Whereditty Geaux a moment den he wuz gone.

Boo:  How bout de great papaw, he still likes dem tropical birds?

Tib:  Oh yes, Flaming Geaux made it too.


3-8

Tib:  Hey Boo, can I borrow your lawnmower.

Boo:  Why sure mah fren but de wife ain't home yet.


3-9

Boo:  Man dis is one good cold beer no?

Tib:  Sure is.  You know your round now.

Boo:  Well you not so skinny yoursef mah fren.


3-10

Boo:  Last nite, I wuz playin wit our youngest, de tree year old, when shes sticks out her finger and sez to me "Daddy, look at dis".  So I sticks her finger in my mouth and sez "Daddys goin to eats you up".  Well she pulls her finger back out really fast and den just stares at her finger.

Tib:  I bets you just scared her huh?

Boo:  It's worse den dat? She den axed me where her booger went.


3-11

Tib:  Dat is one great trophy buck you got dare on de wall.

Boo:  Well I wouldn't call it great.  Dat buck killed my dog Gumbo.

Tib:  I didn't know dat.  Wuz it on de hunt wit you?

Boo:  Oh no.  It fell off de wall and on poor Gumbo.

## 3-12

Tib:  You fraid to die one day Boo?

Boo:  Nope.  But I don't want to be dare when it happens.

## 3-13

Boo:  Man dees mosquitoes are bad today.

Tib:  Sure are, takes all de fun out of fishin.

Boo:  Why didn't dat Noah just swat dose two mosquitoes?

## 3-14

Tib:  Hey buddy, don't walk under dat ladder.

Boo:  You believe in de superstition?

Tib:  Of course.  You don't?

Boo: Awe no way.  It be bad luck to be superstitious.

## 3-15

Tib:  So you takin de family to Disneyworld next summer.

Boo: No way, we went for a week dis summer.  One good ting though, it only rained on us twice.

Tib: Dat sounds ok?

Boo: It rained once for tree days and once for four days.

## 3-16

Tib: So how you did at Evangeline Downs yesterday?

Boo: Oh I bet on a great horse.

Tib: How he did?

Boo: Oh it took seven horses to beat him.


## 3-17

Tib: Man dis beer is good. You know Boo you got somethin in your ear.

Boo: Really. Watts dis? Oh man, it's a suppository. Uh oh.

Tib: Watts wrong?

Boo: I know where my hearin aid is now.


## 3-18

Tib: Sounds like dat cough of yours been cured.

Boo: Sort of. Member I went to doctor every day for a week and nothin worked. Well finally yesterday worked. He gave me a laxative.

Tib: A laxative stopped your coffin?

Boo: Sort of. I be too afraid to cough now.


## 3-19

Boo: Man I feels like I be gettin sick agin today.

Tib:  I tink you be havin dat hypochondria.

Boo:  No but dats probably de only disease I haven't gotten.

***

On April 20th, 2010, the BP licensed Transocean drillin rig Deepwater Horizon exploded and started spewin millions of barrels of oil into the Gulf of Mexico just southeast of Louisiana.  The followin jokes were posted on facebook durin the followin week(s).

3-20

Boo:  Man dis oil spill is goin to ruin Louisiana.

Tib:  I know.  Dat BP needs to axe me how to make dat oil rig stop puttin out.

Boo:  You got an idea?

Tib:  Yep, put a weddin ring on it.

3-21

Tib:  I bet dey can make a car dat runs on water now.

Boo:  How's dat?

Tib:  Well, first, you get water right off de coast of Louisiana, den you...

3-22

Tib:  So how wuz your trip to Grande Isle?

Boo: Not too bad, didn't git to fish none but got to gits some sun on de beach.

Tib: How you did dat wit all dat oil spill.

Boo: Oh it wuz dare. Dose tar balls really hold down your beach blanket nicely.

### 3-23

Boo: It wuz a sad site down on Grande Isle last weekend.

Tib: You saw lots of dead wildlife I'm bettin.

Boo: Dats right. I saw more poor birds in oil dan at Popeye's.

### 3-24

Boo: Sum reporter called de house las night, axes me bout de BP oil spill den if I know de death rate round here.

Tib: Watt you tell her?

Boo: I said I did, one per person.

### 3-25

Tib: So how did de job helpin BP clean up down in Plaquemines Parish go?

Boo: Dey fired me.

Tib: Fired you? I taught day wanted you to help wit de cleanin of de pelicans.

Boo: Dey did.  But after I cleaned and gutted bout 4 dozen of dem, dey got all mad for sum reason and told me to go home.

## 3-26

Tib:  Ok Boo, you need to go tell de plant dat you need to take off two or tree weeks to come wit me to help wit dat oil spill down in Venice.  Go pack your bags.

Boo:  Ok, dat sounds like a plan.  So which is it? I need to know ifin I pack two or tree underwear.

Tib: Hmmm, go wit tree.

\*\*\*

## 3-27

Boo:  I tink I'm goin to donate my body to science.

Tib:  Dats nice of you.

Boo:  Till den, lets have anutter beer.  I need to be preservin dis body in alcohol till den.

## 3-28

Boo:  Nice sittin here on de porch watchin it rain no?

Tib: Sure is but de roof is leakin right on top my head.  Does your roof always leak like dat?

Boo: No, just when it rains.

Boo: Don't you wish you could just drown your troubles away sometimes?

Tib: Sure do mah fren.

Boo: Me too but I can't git de wife to go swimmin.


### 3-30

Boo: De youngest one axes me if I can make sound like a frog today.

Tib: Really, how sweet.

Boo: No not really. I did de frog sounds and den she ran back in house so happy.

Tib: Happy?

Boo: Dats right. I found out later dat mamaw told her dey can all go to Disneyworld when I croak.


### 3-31

Tib: I find de best way to start de day is to jump out of bed, do 25 pushups, den 25 situps. I den jump in de shower and come out and feel Rosy all over.

Boo: Dats interestin. Now tell me more bout dis Rosie.


### 3-32

Tib: So how your Father's day go.

Boo:  Oh mighty fine.  Mah ree, she cooks us up a real nice dinner, my favorite, fried catfish.  And bread puddin for dessert, emhmm emhmmm!

Tib:  Dat sounds good.  You know I tinks dat food has taken place of sex in my life.

Boo:  Me too my mah fren.  I'm goin to put a mirror over our kitchen table next.


## 3-33

Boo:  Oh man, I tink I jus swallowed a catfish bone.

Tib:  Are you chokin?

Boo:  No Tib, I really did.


## 3-34

Tib:  I read las night dat when California became a state sum 160 years ago, de state had no money, most everyone spoke Spanish and dare wuz gunfightin all de time in de streets.

Boo:  Seems nuttin has changed.

Tib:  Seems so.

Boo:  Ceptin de women did have real boobs back den.


## 3-35

Boo:  Tib, could you helps me fill out dees insurance forms?

Tib:  Why sure mah fren.  Let's see here, it axes here if yous ever been in an accident.

Boo:  Nope, don't tink so

Tib:  Not once? Watt bout dat cotton mouth dat bit you last week.

Boo:  You kiddin me, dat wuz no accident.  Dat snake bit me on purpose.


## 3-36

Boo:  So you wants to down to Fred's Bar and drink the night away.

Tib:  Yes sir, I just gots paid and am ready to pass me a good time.

Boo:  Let's gets movin then.

Tib:  Don't you need to axe or tell de wife?

Boo:  Nah, it's easier to axe for forgiveness dan for permission.


## 3-37

Tib:  Well dat wuz sum interestin day in de plant golf tournament for you.

Boo:  I wanna tank you for caddyin for me but you got to be de worse caddie in de world.

Tib:  I don't tinks so Boo, dat would be too much of a coincidence.

## 3-38

Boo:  I wuz walkin down de bayou today and I found dis wallet wit over 200 dollars in it.

Tib:  You goin to return it?

Boo:  I wuz but I den wuz tinkin, ifin I had lost dat money, I would want to be taught a lesson.

## 3-39

Boo:  Oh man, I be hurtin so bad right here just below de belt to de right here.

Tib:  I'm tinkin you got acute appendicitis.

Boo:  Well Ok, tanks, you not so bad lookin yoursef, but watt you tinks bout dis pain?

## 3-40

Tib:  Still no summer job for de oldest boy yet?

Boo:  Well religion is startin to get in de way.

Tib:  How is dat?

Boo:  He won't work if dares a Sunday dat week.

## 3-41

Tib:  Still no job yet for de oldest boy?

Boo:  Oh he works almost everyday now.

Tib:  Dats good no?

Boo: No. He almost works on Monday. He almost works on Tuesday. He almost works on Wednesday...

## 3-42

Tib: So watt you gave Mah ree for her birtday?

Boo: I bought her dis mood ring. When she is in good mood, it turns green.

Tib: So watt happens when she is in bad mood.

Boo: It leaves a red mark on my forehead.

## 3-43

Tib: Happy 4th of July Boo.

Boo: Happy 4th to you too Tib.

Tib: Watts dat you drinkin dare?

Boo: Liber tea mah fren, Liber tea.

## 3-44

Boo: De wife is killin me. Two weeks ago, Mah ree axes me for fifty dollars, last week, she axes for $100. Yesterday, she axes for $150.

Tib: Watt does she do wit all de money?

Boo: I don't know, I never give her any.

## 3-45

Boo: I'm gettin audited today. De accountant sez to wear my worst, oldest clothes. De lawyer sez wear my best suit. Watt you tink?

Tib: Well dare wuz dis bride gettin married and she axed her mom watt to wear on her weddin night, her mom sed wear long underwear head to toe, her best friend sed wear nuttin at all.

Boo: Now watts dat got to do with me.

Tib: No matter watt you wear, you goin to get screwed.


## 3-46

Tib: Ifin you won de lottery, would you quit your job at de plant.

Boo: Oh no, I wouldn't be like dose utter lottery winners and quit my job. I would make de plant manager's life a livin hell for de first week or two.


## 3-47

Tib: You never done told me how you did at de races lass night?

Boo: Well you know it wuz July 7th, I found myself sittin in seat 7, row 7, section 7. De 7th race had a horse named Mickey Mantle, member his number wuz 7. So I bet all my money on dat horse.

Tib: So how did he do?

Boo: Came in 7th.

Tib: Why you look so down in de dumps mah fren?

Boo: Well member last month my Aunt Jackie left me $1000 when she passed away.

Tib: Oh yes, I member dat.

Boo: Well a week later, a distant cousin passed away left me $200. A week after dat a second couzan passed and left me one hundred dollars.

Tib: So dats why you be upset?

Boo: Yep, dis week, nuttin.

3-49

Tib: Boo, mind me axin you if yall ever do it doggie style?

Boo: No, my Mah ree is more into de trick dog style.

Tib: Man dat sounds a bit kinky no?

Boo: Fraid not, whenever I make a move, she rolls over and plays dead.

3-50

Tib: What time it is?

Boo: Lets see here, hmmm, it be 7:30 now.

Tib: Dat is sum nice pocket watch you got dare. Where you got dat?

Boo: I got dis antique from great papaw on his deathbed.

Tib:  Dat wuz nice gift of him.

Boo:  Oh no, he put up hell of a fight for it.


## 3-51

Boo:  Can't go fishin next wit you next weekend.  My Mah ree won't let me go.

Tib:  Dats too bad, Ima goin to pass a good time wit out cha anyways.  You stay home wit your Cleopatra you "Bootus".

Boo:  Yeah, wit my very own queen of denial.


## 3-52

Tib:  I reads here dat a single catfish can produce over a thousand offspring.

Boo:  Man dats someting.  Just tink how many de married ones have.


## 3-53

Tib:  So how wuz your trip Sea World in San Antonio wit de family.

Boo:  Oh it wuz nice.  I got to see dem circumcise one dem killer whales dare.

Tib:  Really.  How do you circumcise a whale?

Boo:  Dey sent down dees four skin divers.

## 3-54

Boo:  Heard ol Uncle Homer is gettin married?

Tib:  Dat ole cuss, he musta be sum 80 years old now, why he wanta git married?

Boo:  Who sed he wanted to.

## 3-55

Boo:  Man my whole body be hurtin.

Tib:  Your whole body?

Boo:  Watch, I touch my leg, Aiyee!, My forehead, Aiyee!, My chest, ouch! My arm, Aiyee!

Tib:  Your finger be broken mah fren.

## 3-56

Boo:  Man I got dat song "She's a lady" stuck on my mind.

Tib:  You got de Tom Jones syndrome.

Boo:  Really? Is it common?

Tib:  It's not unusual.

## 3-57

Tib:  Started takin vitamins dis week to make me more healthy.

Boo:  Vitamins? I tried dat once, didn't like it.

Tib:  Watt wuz wrong wit it?

Boo:  Got tired of dem.  Too expensive too.  I had to eat so many of dem before I got full.


## 3-58

Tib:  Dat wuz sum good pork sausage you bar b qued yesterdey.

Boo:  Yep.

Tib:  You know it takes 10 pigs to make 1000 sausages.

Boo:  Dats amazin watt dey can teach dem.


## 3-59

Boo:  Awe Tib, who gave you dat black eye.

Tib:  Nobody.  I had to fight for it.


## 3-60

Boo:  Say you had a green ball in one hand and a green ball in de utter hand, watt would you have?

Tib:  Hmmm, de gator's undivided attention?


## 3-61

Tib:  You member Buckwheat from de Our Gang show.

Boo:  Ah yes, he wuz one my favorites on de show.  He still alive?

Tib:  Yep and he's converted to Isalm.

Boo:  Oh no.

Tib:  His new name is Kareem of Wheat.


## 3-62

Tib:  Watt you tink is man's greatest invention.

Boo:  Oh I'm guessin electricity.

Tib:  Yep, dat could be it.

Boo:  If there weren't no lectricity, we'd be watchin dis Sportscenter on de tv by candle light.


## 3-63

Tib:  Dat Nick Saban be mad at dem sport agents for takin advantage of his football players, callin dem pimps.

Boo:  Really? So what cha call a person who breaks promises and leaves a bunch of LSU football players to go make more money at Miami den lies and leaves dose players to make more money at Bama.

Tib:  A whore?

Boo:  Hack, cough, hack...Excuse me I'm chokin on de irony of it all.


## 3-64

Tib:  Dey talkin bout goin de metric system agin.

Boo:  No, you kiddin right?

Tib:  Nope, I read bout it in de paper dis mornin.

Boo:  Ifin God wanted us to be metric, he would have appointed 10 apostles instead of 12.


## 3-65

Boo:  Can you believe dat Bordelon down de bayou wuz caught bein married to two women.

Tib:  No way!

Boo:  Yes way, he had his Kate here and dare wuz dis Edith woman in Baton Rouge.

Tib:  So he wanted to have his Kate and Edith too.


## 3-66

Boo:  I got Mah ree all sick, my truck done broke down, I need a new outboard engine for de boat, just so many tings to deal wit.

Tib:  Member God never gives you more den you can handle.

Boo:  Yes I know dat but I wish he didn't trust me so much sumtimes.


## 3-67

Tib:  Hows your week been wit de mother-in-law stayin over?

Boo:  Oh pretty good, not too bad.  Las night she actually gave me a compliment.

Tib:  No way! Watt she say?

Boo:  She called me a perfect idiot.

### 3-68

Boo:  Dat wuz one good lookin woman I saw you wit last night at Fred's bar.

Tib:  Dat she wuz.

Boo:  Reminds me of a parkin ticket.

Tib:  How's dat?

Boo:  She had fine written all over her.

### 3-69

Tib:  See how de end of de road dare looks like dares water sittin on it?

Boo:  Yes I sees it, looks like dares a lake on it.

Tib:  Dats watt dey call an optical illusion.

Boo:  Dats no optical illusion Tib, it just looks likes one.

### 3-70

Tib:  Hey Boo, you gots a CD burner?

Boo:  Sure do my friend.

Tib:  Can I come by tomorrow and use it?

Boo:  Why sure, just give me a little warnin when you're comin so I can start up de fireplace.

## 3-71

Tib:  You tink old men wear boxers or shorts?

Boo:  Well dat Depends.

Tib:  You know dem pants are lookin a bit tight on you dare.

Boo:  Yes, as you can see, food is startin to replace sex in my life.  I can't even get into my own pants.

## 3-72

Boo:  So watt you want to do?

Tib:  Oh don't know.

Boo:  Come on Tib, come up wit sometin.

Tib:  Ok, I been readin bout dis meditation, we could try meditation.

Boo:  Whatever, I'm sure it beats sittin round here doin nuttin.

## 3-73

Tib:  Did you hear bout dat near miss of dose planes in Baton Rouge yesterday?

Boo:  Sure did.

Tib:  Pretty scary no?

Boo:  I wonder why dey don't call it a near hit?

## 3-74

Tib:  Tell me, where you tink right now is de most dangerous place in de U.S.?

Boo:  Ok, how bout New Awlens?

Tib:  Nope.

Boo:  New York?

Tib:  Nope.

Boo:  Baton Rouge?

Tib:  Nope.

Boo:  Ok, where it is?

Tib:  De most dangerous place to be in de U.S.  now is between a Republican and a votin booth.


## 3-75

Tib:  You finally got your youngest one to sleep.

Boo:  Yep, just now, be quiet ok.

Tib:  Watt you do?

Boo:  I told her one of our Cajun fairy tales.

Tib:  I didn't know bout Cajun fairy tales.  Dey different from de "Once upon a time" fairy tales?

Boo:  Sort of, same story but ours starts wit "You ain't goin to believe dis S@#$".

3-76

Tib: You tink you can name all de ten commandments?

Boo: Of course, you want me to name dem, do you care watt order?

Tib: Doesn't matter to me.

Boo: Ok den. 5,3,1,7,8,9,2,4,10 and den 6.


3-77

Tib: Why wouldn't you dance wit one dem two girls I met at Fred's bar las night.

Boo: Oh didn't want to look like idiot in front everyone dare.

Tib: You got watt dey call an inferiority complex my friend. Anyway, we all have sum level of inferiority in us.

Boo: Well I bet my inferiority complex isn't as good as yours.


3-78

Boo: I tried cheer up Beniot down de bayou. He been depressed cuz he found his wife in bed wit one of de Mouton boys.

Tib: Dats tough.

Boo: I sed he needed to git over it, it ain't de end of de world. Well he den axes me watt I would do ifin I caught a man in bed wit my Mah ree.

Tib: Watt you say to dat?

Boo: I sed I would break his little white stick den I would have gone over and kicked his seein eye dog.

Boo:  I'm tired of gettin in trouble for goin to Fred's bar, I ain't goin back no more.

Tib:  Now Boo, there ain't no reason to use no double negatives you know, not never.

Boo:  Ok, I don't need no lessons from you.


3-80

Boo:  I'm guessin you be right bout us walkin home from Fred's bar tonight.

Tib:  Yes, we both had a few too many.

Boo:  Tell you dis, when I get home, first ting I'ma goin do is tear off my Mah ree's underwear.

Tib:  Feelin a bit frisky no?

Boo:  No, de elastic is killin me.


3-81

Boo:  Tib, check out dat blond at end of de bar.  Watt you do if she came over here and kissed you.

Tib:  Oh I would kiss her back.  You?.

Boo:  I would kiss her front.


3-82

Boo:  Gotta take Mah ree to de doctor to git sum more birth control pills.  Dey make us sleep better.

Tib:  Sleep better? How do dey do dat?

Boo:  She puts dem in our oldest daughter's coffee in de mornin.

### 3-83

Tib:  Dey got 32 ounce Keystone Light beers at Fred's bar for a dollar today.

Boo:  Oh no not for me, I'll stick wit my Bud Light.

Tib:  But 32 ounces is a lot of beer for a dollar no?

Boo:  Look here, I wants quality, not quantity my friend, and lots of it.

### 3-84

Boo:  My Mah ree and me had de sex nearly every night dis week.

Tib:   Dats so.  Good for you.

Boo:  We nearly had sex Monday night, we nearly had sex Tuesday night...

### 3-85

Boo:  Seems you been wit dat pretty little lady from Fred's you met last weekend all dis week.

Tib:  Dats right.

Boo:  Been sowin your oats everyday dis week no?

Tib:  I guess so.  I'll be goin to Mass today and prayin.

Boo:  Prayin for watt?

Tib:  Crop failure.


### 3-86

Tib:  I been wonderin.  Who you tink enjoys de sex better, men or women.

Boo:  Oh us men of course.  Dats why we be so obsessed bout it.

Tib:  You tink so? Watt bout dis then.  Say your ear itches. Watt you do?

Boo:  Well I puts a finger in it and wiggle it round.

Tib:  Ahh exactly.  So which feels better after, your ear or your finger?


### 3-87

Boo:  Did you have any luck wit dat fine young lady at Fred's bar last night.

Tib:  Nope, it wuz over as soon as I axed her watt her sign wuz.

Boo:  Watt wuz her sign?

Tib:  Do not enter.


### 3-88

Boo:  Tib, I found tree hand grenades in pa paw's shed.  I tink I'll bring dem down to de Sheriff's office.

Tib:  Hmmm, not sure bout dat.  Watt if one of dem blows up?

Boo:  Well I'll just tell dem I found two den.

Boo:  How bout you and me go in halves and get pa paw a hooker for his birtday.

Tib:  Your pa paw be 92 den.  Prolonged sex wit a girl could be fatal.

Boo:  Oh well, if she dies, she dies.

Boo:  You heard dat pa paw got dat hooker we got for him pregnant.

Tib:  Really.  Let me tell you dis story.  Say I went fishin and I forgot my gun.  Dis gator comes up to our bateau.  I grab my fishin pole and shoot it through de head.  Hows dat?

Boo:  Dats not possible.  Sumbody else must of done shot dat gator.

Tib:  Dats my point exactly.

Boo:  I accidently broke a mirror las night, now I got seven years bad luck.

Tib:  Why don't you call Sotile.

Boo:  De lawyer, why?

Tib:  Maybe he can get you five.

Tib:  You and Mah ree married close to 25 years now no?

Boo:  Dats right.

Tib:  And she still let's you pretty much go drinkin or fishin whenever you want to no?.

Boo: Dats right.  I done found someone dat I really love and wanted to be close to and would leave me alone.


### 3-93

Boo:  I tried dat toilet brush de wife keeps in de bathroom today.

Tib:  Work good no?

Boo:  No, I'm goin back to de toilet paper.


### 3-94

Boo:  Got to take de wife goin to de gynecologist today for her annual check up.

Tib:  Dis guyno a man or woman?

Boo:  Oh she be a woman doctor.

Tib:  Really, seems most women like only a man guyno lookin dare.

Boo:  I taught so too and axed her bout it.  She says dat goin to male guyno is like goin to an auto mechanic dat don't even own a car.

3-95

Boo:  Man dis gettin old aint worth nuttin.  I be forgettin names, den faces.  Now I'm forgettin to pull my zipper up.

Tib:  Well dats not dat bad.  It's when you start forgettin to pull it down.

3-96

Tib:  Read some of dis book las night, sed dat men and women come from different planets.

Boo:  Oh I figured dat out after I got married.

Tib:  How long did dat take?

Boo:  Oh after 15 or 20 minutes.

3-97

Boo:  Watt's de name of dat book you been readin bout women comin from nutter planet?

Tib:  Men are from Mars, Women are from Venus.

Boo:  Well you need to read de book I be writtin.

Tib:  Watts it's name?

Boo:  Women are from Venus, Men are wrong.

Boo: Did you know dat Obama gots a dog named Bo?

Tib: I knowed dat, but dares a big difference between dat dog and Obama.

Boo: Watts dat?

Tib: De dog has papers.

Boo: Paper sez dat lots of dealers resold some of de "Cash for Clunkers" cars dey got. Dey wuz supposed to jumk dem.

Tib: Dat figures. Dare wuz one ting good about dat stupid program.

Boo: Watts dat?

Tib: It got most dem Obama stickers off de road.

Tib: Watched your boy playin baseball today. Sum impressive. I didn't know he wuz a switch hitter.

Boo: Yep, he can hit and throw with either arm.

Tib: I'd give my right arm to be ambidextrous like dat.

Tib: Boo I hates to admit it but dat oldest daughter of yours sure be a looker. Bet she gots lots of boys chasin her.

Boo: Yes, she is a beauty. I did axe her if she wuz sexually active.

Tib: You did? Watt she say?

Boo: She said no.

Tib: Dats good no?

Boo: No. Den she said, "I just lie dare."

# A little lagniappe 1

Boo:  You should see de list of words dey got my youngest spose to learn watt dey mean.

Tib:  Go ahead, axe me dem, let's see how I do.

Boo:  Artery

Tib:  De study of paintins

Boo:  Barium

Tib:  Watt dey do at de cemetery

Boo:  Cauterize

Tib:  Made de eyes at a pretty woman

Boo:  Dialate

Tib:  To live long time


# A little lagniappe 2

Tib:  Go on, keep axen me dose definition words your son gots from school

Boo:  Enema

Tib:  Not our friend

Boo:  Nitrates

Tib:  Cheaper den day rates

Boo:  Node

Tib:  To know watt it means

Boo:  Urine

Tib:  Opposite of you're out

Boo:  Varicose

Tib:  Right nearby

Boo:  Man you're sum good Tib.

## A little lagniappe 3

Boo:  De oldest boy been hammerin me to buy him a truck. Tired of walkin to work.

Tib:  You goin to one day?

Boo:  Of course but I told him dat he had to get his long hair cut first den we talk bout it.  Den he goes off bout Moses, Jesus, Samson all havin long hair.

Tib: Tough argument dare, watt you say to dat?

Boo: I reminded him dat dey walked everywhere too.

## A little lagniappe 4

Tib:  So you never told me how your little one did wit his spellin test.

Boo:  Oh he did good but teacher got upset with one word.

Tib:  He got it wrong?

Boo: No, he spelled de word "straight" right.  But den when she axes him de definition, he sed "Without water".

## A little lagniappe 5

Boo: Look at dis, I bought dis nice round rug for de camp on sale. Salesman told me it wuz in perfect condition. Now look here, dares a hole in de middle.

Tib: You sure he didn't say "mint" condition?

## A little lagniappe 6

Tib: Do you know when wuz Rome built?

Boo: At night.

Tib: At night? Why you say dat?

Boo: Cuz papaw always sed dat Rome wuzn't built in a day.

## A little lagniappe 7

Boo: Man I got to speak to my youngest daughter's class on career day tomorrow. You got any advice?

Tib: Make sure you have a good beginnin and a good endin and keep de two of dem as close as possible.

Boo: Ha ha. Anyting else?

Tib: Just like I sed, keep it short. If you don't strike oil in 2 minutes, quit boring.

## 4-1

Tib:  So how it went at your daughter's career day?  How wuz your speech?

Boo:  I didn't git to give it.  Sum kid's politician dad started talkin and wouldn't stop.  I finally walked out.

Tib:  Watt he talk bout all dat time?

Boo:  He didn't say.

Tib:  Wasted no words no?

Boo:  Nope, used every one of them.

## 4-2

Boo:  I don't understand de deal wit vegans I read bout, watts dare problem?

Tib:  Dey don't want us eatin animals.

Boo:  If God had not wanted us to eat animals, he wouldn't have made dem with meat.

## 4-3

Boo:  I heard of Murphy's law but I don't know watt dis Cole's Law is, you know?

Tib:  Well, Murphy's law is anyting dat can go wrong will go wrong, de utter is thin sliced cabbage.

4-4

Boo: Dey say dat a sign for too much stress is eatin too much and drinkin too much.

Tib: Sounds like my idea of de perfect day.

4-5

Boo: Man it's wuz sum hot yesterday no. I saw two trees fightin over a dog.

Tib: Dats nuttin. I saw a bird usin a pot holder to grab de worm.

Boo: It's so hot dat my potatoes are alreadin done in de ground, just needs sum salt, pepper and butter now.

Tib: I'm feedin my chickens ice to keep dem from layin boiled eggs.

Boo: Man it's sum hot.

Tib: Yes it is mah fren.

4-6

Boo: Hey you know the difference between one of dem Northern zoos and ours down here?

Tib: Hmmm, don't know, dey all seem to be same ting to me.

Boo: Well ours has a recipe listed next to de animal name.

4-7

Boo: Tib say you have two new hummers, would you give me one?

Tib: Definitely.

Boo: Say you got two of dem cigarette boats, would you give me one?

Tib: Sure ting mah fren.

Boo: So watt if you had two shot guns, would you give me one?

Tib: Nope.

Boo: You give me a hummer, a boat, but no shotgun. Watt de difference?

Tib: De difference is you know I got two shotguns.

4-8

Boo: I watched dat new Superman movie las night. Watched him stop a bullet wit his eye.

Tib: De man can stop bullets wit his eye but he always ducks when dey throw a gun at him.

4-9

Tib: You still fightin moths in de house?

Boo: Yep and dose stupid moth balls you told me bout, well dey be worthless.

Tib: Dat didn't git rid of dem?

110

Boo:  You know how hard it is to hit a moth with one dem balls.

### 4-10

Boo:  Mah ree wuz up till 4AM las night.

Tib:  Watts she doin till 4AM?

Boo:  Waitin for us to git home from Fred's bar.

### 4-11

Tib:  You heard dat Beth and sum of de utter ladies went to beach dis weekend.

Boo:  Yep, Mah ree sed dat sum naked man ran up on dem on de beach and dat Lisa and Kelly had a stroke.

Tib:  I'm guessin Beth couldn't reach?

### 4-12

Boo:  Dat wuz sum ugly woman I saw you wit las night at Fred's bar.

Tib:  Awe, she wuzn't dat bad.

Boo:  Fren. She should have to have a license to be dat ugly.

Tib:  You exaggerate.

Boo:  No, I bet my dog would hump her leg wit his eyes closed.

Tib:  Dats enuff ok.

Boo: I bet dat baboon wants his ass back.

## 4-13

Boo: Dat girl wuz sum ugly I saw you wit at Fred's.

Tib: She wuzn't dat bad.

Boo: Her picture looked as if she had a hobby of steppin on rakes.

Tib: Well de camera just caught her worst side dats all.

Boo: Right, if you call her worst side de outside.

Tib: Well she looked good in de moon light.

Boo: Total darkness does suit her better.

## 4-14

Boo: Dat girl you wuz wit at Fred's had dat faraway look, de farther away, de better she looked.

Tib: Ok ok, maybe she wuzn't perfect.

Boo: Dat girl wuz born ugly mah fren. And built to las.

Tib: I bet you been to bed wit an ugly woman before.

Boo: Nope, never, not me mah fren. Now I have woken up wit sum.

## 4-15

Boo: Dat girl you wuz wit at Fred's so ugly, dat her shadow quit.

Tib:  Nuff already.

Boo:  Ifin she had been a scarecrow, de corn would have run away.

Tib:  Ha ha.

Boo:  Even dat Elephant man would have paid to see her. She's so ugly you would have to take her to work.

Tib:  Whys dat?

Boo:  So you wouldn't have to kiss her good bye.


### 4-16

Boo:  Oh my achin head, I'm quittin de drinkin and gamblin from now on.

Tib:  Ha, you sed dat bout four or five months ago too, member dat.

Boo:  Oh dat time.  Dat wuz cuz I heard bout "Crisis in de Gulf" and figured him bein dat close, I better start bein good.


### 4-17

Boo:  Well las night Mah ree tells de youngest bout makin babies.

Tib:  Well be bout dat age I guess.

Boo:  She den axes Mah ree bout kittens, so Mah ree tells her it's same as wit babies.

Tib:  And so?

Boo:  Den she ran up and gave me a big hug and sed "My daddy can do anyting".

## 4-18

Tib: De Tigers whooped up on dem Aggies las night no?

Boo: Yep, dey sure did mah fren.

Tib: Man dem tigers sum big and strong players no? You tinks us normal people are gettin stronger too?

Boo: Oh I tinks so. I member barely bein able to carry $10 worth of groceries home turty years ago, now my youngest one can carry dat much wit one hand.

## 4-19

Boo: Looks like de middle child done moved from child to grown up now.

Tib: How you know dat?

Boo: It's when dey stop axin you where dey came from and start refusin to tell you where dey goin.

## 4-20

Boo: De oldest boy movin back in, done lost his job agin.

Tib: You know dat us humans are de only creatures dat let dare young ones come back home.

Boo: Dat be true, never taught of dat. How you be so wise all de time?

Tib: Oh it be easy. Just tink of sumting stupid to say, den don't say it.

Boo: I gots me one dem lectric toothbrushes from de dentist yesterday.

Tib: Been wantin to git one, how it works?

Boo: Well good ceptin I accidently left it on all night las night.

Tib: All night?

Boo: Yes, and you wouldn't believe how clean de bathroom is now.

Boo: Bad day today.

Tib: Whys dat?

Boo: I woke up and found dat our waterbed done sprung a leak.

Tib: You don't have no waterbed?

Boo: I know.

Boo: De wife caught me suckin in my stomach when I wuz weighin myself las night. She had sum laugh.

Tib: Suckin in your stomach is not goin to help.

Boo: Well it's de only way I can see de numbers.

## 4-24

Boo:  Whatcha got in de bag dare Tib?

Tib:  Oh dats sum old clothes I'm donatin to help de starvin people round de world.  You ought to donate too.

Boo:  Oh I don't tink so.

Tib:  Why not?

Boo:  Cuz anyone dat can fit in my clothes ain't starvin.


## 4-25

Boo:  Well LSU playin Tennessee dis weekend, tink we can beat dem?

Tib:  Oh yes, dat reminds me.  How many freshman Tennessee players it takes to change a light bulb?

Boo:  Hmmm, don't know?

Tib:  None.  Cuz dats a sophomore class at Tennessee.


## 4-26

Boo:  Haw, we done stole a win las night didn't we.  And dats sum ugly orange dem Tennessee players be wearin.

Tib:  Dats right but dares a good reason for it.  It makes sense to me.

Boo: How's dat?

Tib: Well dey can wear for de game Saturday, huntin on Sunday, and pickin up trash on de highway rest of de week.

## 4-27

Tib:  I heard you helped de Sheriff today lookin for dat escaped murderer from Angola.  De one dat drowned in Vermillion bay.  So no luck findin him?

Boo:  Dey didn't find him but I did, and guess watt.  He had 24 of de prettiest blue crabs you ever done saw clingin to him.  You want sum?

Tib:  Yes sir ree.  So why I hear dey still lookin for him?

Boo:  I didn't tell dem.  I figured I'd tell dem after gettin a nutter batch of crabs tomorrow.

## 4-28

Boo:  I noticed at de plant dat all us grunt plant workers talk bout football.  Our supervisors talk bout tennis.  De managers, dey all talk bout golf.  Watt do you make of dat?

Tib:  Seems de higher up you are, de smaller your balls are.

## 4-29

Boo:  Saw dis guy on tv las night dat had tattoos of Ronald Reagan on one butt cheek and one of George Bush on de utter.

Tib:  Really?  So he didn't have one of our current president?

Boo:  Oh I saw it.  It was in de middle.

## 4-30

Tib:  Uh oh, how you got dat new black eye dare?

Boo:  Well I made mistake of goin shoppin wit de wife.  She wuz lookin to buy a new bathin suit since dey be on sale now.  She axed me if she should git a bikini or a all-in-one.  I sed she should git de bikini.

Tib:  And you got black eye for dat?

Boo:  No I got de black eye after I sed she wuz never git it all in one.

## 4-31

Boo:  You know I tink we should always give 100% at work.

Tib:  Really?  Dat doesn't sound like you.  So how you do dat?

Boo:  Well I figure I give 12% on Monday, 23% on Tuesday, 40% Wednesday, 20% Thursday, and den 5% on Fridays.

## 4-32

Boo:  Sez in de paper dat dare be sum 25 million Americans not workin now.

Tib:  Just tink how many dare would be if dey counted de ones wit jobs.

## 4-33

Tib:  So tell me why you always got dat piece of rope hangin on your porch here.

Boo:  Well mah fren, dats my always reliable weather predictor.

Tib:  Now how does dat work?

Boo:  It works great.  If it be swingin it be windy, if it be wet, it be rainin.


### 4-34

Tib:  Sez in de paper here is dat time is essential part of de measurin system used to sequence events, to compare de durations of events and de intervals between dem, and to quantify de motions of objects.

Boo:  And all dis time I taught it wuz watt kept everyting from happenin at once.


### 4-35

Boo:  Las nite I walks into de bedroom wit just my new boots on.

Tib:  Did she notice dem?

Boo:  No, she sed she didn't see anyting different.  Den she sed, "It wuz hangin down las nite, it's hangin down tonight, and it'll be hangin down tomorrow".  So I sez to her "Little Boo is hangin down cuz he be lookin at my new boots!"

Tib:  Ha!  So watt she say to dat?

Boo:  She sed I should have bought a hat.


### 4-36

Boo:  Man dees prunes dey got here at Fred's bar are sum good.

Tib:  You eatin dem like peanuts, you better slow down.

Boo:  Why?  Dey cheap.

Tib:  Man who eat many prunes gits a good run for his money.

### 4-37

Boo:  Come on in Tib, I'm goin to bar b que sum chicken.

Tib:  Dats sounds good.  How did you prepare de chicken?

Boo:  Well I didn't.  I just tell dem right den they goin to die.

### 4-38

Boo:  De oldest in high school, scored 25 on her SAT test, believe dat?

Tib:  Dat is pretty good.  I member score I tink bout 20 or 21. Watt did you git on your SAT?

Boo:  Drool.

### 4-39

Boo:  Aw man, we done stayed way too long here at Fred's bar tonight.

Tib:  Dat we did.  Our heads goin to be hurtin tomorrow.

Boo:  I'm goin to hate myself in de mornin.

Tib:  Not if you sleep till noon like me.

Boo:  De voices in my head keep tellin me we need to move down de bayou a ways further to catch de fish.

Tib:  Dis spot right here will pay off I'm tellin you.  You need to stop listen to de voices in your head.

Boo:  Aw you're just jealous cuz de voices are talkin to just me.

4-41

Tib:  Uh oh, why de black eye after your wife's birtday las night.

Boo:  Well earlier in de week, she had dis dream bout me givin her a 1 carat diamond ring.  She axes watt dat means.  I tell her she'll find out on her birtday.

Tib:  You got a black eye for givin her a ring?

Boo:  No.  It wuz when I gave her a book, "De Meanin of Dreams".

4-42

Tib:  Ok nuff beer for me, let's go git sometin to eat.  How bout sum Chinese.

Boo:  Naw, an hour later we will be hungry agin.

Tib:  Ok, how bout sum Italian?

Boo:  Naw, an hour later we will still be eatin.

## 4-43

Boo: Can you believe de wife paid sum $30 for a little bitty jar of face cream. Sez it makes her beautiful.

Tib: Well you can't hold dat against her no?

Boo: You know for half dat amount I could git a case of cheap beer dat does de same ting.

## 4-44

Boo: Man I didn't know dat Obama wuz a Right to Lifer.

Tib: I don't tink so.

Boo: He is due to dat new health care bill he done passed. Dare be long waitin lists for all de health care services.

Tib: So how does dat make Obama a right to lifer?

Boo: Dares a nine month waitin list for abortions now.

## 4-45

Boo: So tell me watt exactly does dis "recession" mean?

Tib: To put it simple mah fren, it like when your neighbor loses his job.

Boo: And "depression"?

Tib: Dats when you lose your job.

Boo: And den watt is "recovery"?

Tib: Dats when Obama loses his job.

Boo:  I saw a car load of lawyers done drove into de bayou.

Tib:  Really?

Boo:  Dats right.  Bein I don't hold nuttin against lawyers, I notified de sheriff bout it.

Tib:  So dey ok now?

Boo:  Well I rode by just a while ago and de car wuz still dare. Seems I wasted a stamp.

4-47

Boo:  I reads dat Obama wants to make de tax forms simpler for us citizens.

Tib:  I know how he can test dem.

Boo:  How's dat?

Tib:  Test dem on dat Joe Biden.

4-48

Tib:  Man las night while I wuz walkin home I taught I saw a ghost.

Boo:  No way!  Watt you do?

Tib:  Well I tried to reach out an touch it.

Boo:  Den watt happened?

Tib:  I got a hand full of sheet.

## 4-49

Boo:  Sum places had Halloween las night.  Sum goin to have it Monday night.  Watt day you tink Halloween should be on?

Tib:  Halloween.

## 4-50

Boo:  De lawyer for de plant had a baby girl today.  Dey lookin for girl's name.  You got any ideas.

Tib:  How bout Sue.

## 4-51

Tib:  You know de difference between unlawful and illegal?

Boo:  Well lets see, one means it be against de law, de utter one is a sick bird.

## 4-52

Boo:  Man I hates dat Nancy Pelosi toilet paper de wifey bought.

Tib:  Nancy Pelosi toilet paper?

Boo:  It's rough, and it's tough, and it don't take no crap off nobody.

Tib:  Good riddance to her too, way to geaux America.

Boo:  De lawyer at de plant didn't like your suggestion of "Sue" for his new baby girl.  Sed dat his wife is Japanese and dat just didn't fit.

Tib:  How bout "Sosumi" den.


## 4-54

Tib:  Do you know watt a Freudian slip is?

Boo:  Dats when you say one ting but you meant your mother.


## 4-55

Tib:  You want to grab a few beers down at Fred's bar.

Boo:  Sure lets go.

Tib:  You want to axe de wife if she wants to go?

Boo:  No way.  Dats like axin de game warden to go fishin.


## 4-56

Boo:  Dat wuz sum game las night, LSU done beat Bama and Satan, I mean Saban.

Tib:  Sure wuz.  But I still worry bout Les Miles's clock management.

Boo:  Why?  Didn't hurt him dis game?

Tib:  So watts he goin to do for de daylights time change dis weekend?

Boo:  Ahh, good question.  I suspect he left dat to de wife.

## 4-57

Tib:  Hey I never noticed dat horseshoe nailed up over your porch here?

Boo:  Yeah.  Hung dat a few years ago, brings me good luck.

Tib:  I never knew you believed in superstition.

Boo:  Oh I don't believes in it.  But it works whether you believes it or not.

## 4-58

Tib:  Say you could have a conversation wit sumone, livin or dead, who would dat be?

Boo:  Dats easy, de livin one.

## 4-59

Boo:  Man I been arguin wit de wife all day today.

Tib:  Be careful dare Boo.  Man who fight wit wife all day git no piece at night.

## 4-60

Tib:  So did you git de loan you wanted to git dat new bass boat.

Boo:  No.  Dey wouldn't give it to me.  Sed dat I didn't qualify for it.

Tib:  Isn't it funny how de banks will only loan money to people dat can prove dey don't need it.

## 4-61

Tib:  Boo, you bests slow down dare.  Dats liked de sixth or seventh beer you had since we got to Fred's here.

Boo:  Hey I'm fine.  You know in dog beers, dis is still my first one.

## 4-62

Boo:  You member me scorin 4 touchdowns against Breaux Bridge our senior year.

Tib:  Shore do.  You were quite de all around athlete back den.

Boo:  Yes I wuz.

Tib:  Now you're just all round.

## 4-63

Boo:  Hey Tib, I never noticed you wearin an earring before. How long you been wearin it?

Tib:  Ever since de girlfriend found it in my truck.

## 4-64

Tib:  My woman laughed durin our makin love las night.  Does your Mah ree ever laugh durin sex.

Boo:  Oh yes, all de time.  Doesn't matter watt she's readin.


### 4-65

Boo:  I member learnin to swim when I was little.  Dat crazy Hebert walked me down to end of pier den told me to jump. I wuz little and I wuz scared of de snakes and gators den. Den he threaten to ram me wit his manhood if I didn't jump.

Tib:  So did you jump?

Boo:  Yes, a little bit at first.


### 4-66

Tib:  Why you got dat sign sayin "Beware of parakeet" on your fence.  Since when dat pet bird your boy got to be so dangerous?

Boo:  Since when dat pet bird can whistle for our pet pit bull.


### 4-67

Tib:  Dat new Hebert grandchild sum ugly baby no?

Boo:  Momma sed I wuz an ugly baby.

Tib:  Watt a terrible ting to say to your own son.

Boo:  Worse.  She sed dat she didn't breast feed me neither cuz she only liked me as a friend.

Tib: You heard dat ol lady Simoneaux done caught de mad cow disease. Don't know bout her husband Will.

Boo: Well he don't have to worry, he can't git it.

Tib: Why not?

Boo: Cuz were all pigs.

Boo: Saw dis bumper sticker today but don't know watt it means?

Tib: Watt it sed?

Boo: Boycott shampoo. Watt you tink dat means?

Tib: Dey want real poo?

Tib: Ok dats nuff beer. Lets have a shot of tequila.

Boo: Tequila. Don't know bout dat.

Tib: Come on, it will put sum lead in your pencil.

Boo: Dat might be true but I gots nobody to write to.

Tib: Wuz watchin dat Discovery channel bout scuba divin. I wonder why dey always fall off backwards off de boat.

Boo: Tib you sum dumb coonass, if dey fall front ways dey would still be in de boat.

## 4-72

Tib: Saw dis homeless man by de interstate today. He sed he hadn't eatin in two days.

Boo: Man, I wish I had his will power.

## 4-73

Tib: Check out de babe at de end of de bar dare.

Boo: Aiyiyii! Dats sum looker no?

Tib: I'd liked to take her home and do her turkey style.

Boo: Yea me too...watt? Watt is turkey style?

Tib: Gobble, gobble, gobble.

## 4-74

Tib: I see you done cooked 2 turkeys dare.

Boo: Yep. Dis fried one is actually de son of dis one dat wuz roasted.

Tib: Oh if de ol papa turkey could see him now, he'd turn over in his gravy.

Boo:  Well good mornin Tib, I hope you had a nice Tanksgivin.

Tib:  Knock knock.

Boo:  Okay, who dat?

Tib:  Arthur.

Boo:  Arthur who?

Tib:  Arthur any leftovers?

Boo:  Doctor sez I got dis heart murmur.  Sez I got to cut my sex life by half.  But I don't know which half to give up?

Tib:  Half?

Boo:  Yes.  De lookin or de thinkin.

Tib:  I see your in-laws are finally gone from dare Tanksgivin visit.

Boo:  Yep.  Took dem to de airport dis mornin.  Dey leave tomorrow.

Tib:  Looks like your youngest girl dare has quite a doll collection.

Boo:  She wants de "divorced Barbie" doll for Christmas dis year.

Tib:  Never heard of dat one.

Boo: Oh yes, saves a lot of time.  It comes wit all of Ken's stuff already.

### 4-79

Boo:  De middle one wants to play in de school band.  You know de difference between a fiddle and a cello?

Tib:  A cello will burn longer.

### 4-80

Tib:  Do you ever wake up grumpy in de mornin?

Boo:  Oh no.  I let her sleep.

### 4-81

Boo:  Honey, can you tell ifin a man be well hung or not?

Mah ree:  Yes my dear.  It's when you can barely git a finger between de neck and de noose.

### 4-82

Tib:  You heard dat Aucoin down de bayou broke his leg in two places.

Boo:  Really.  He needs to quit goin to dose places.

Tib:  Sez in de paper de shortest sentence in de English language is "I am".

Boo:  I bet I know de longest one.

Tib:  Watts dat?

Boo:  "I do".

Boo:  You know Tib, it only takes one drink to git me drunk.

Tib:  Ha, dats true.  Problem is dat we don't know if it's de 14th or 15th beer.

Boo:  Well de wife be drivin me to drink.

Tib:  You lucky mah fren.  I had to walk here.

Boo:  I gits home from las night and de wife sez she got good news and bad news bout my truck.

Tib:  Uh oh.

Boo:  Dats how I felt.  I sez to her, just give me de good news.

Tib:  Watt she say?

Boo:  Dat de airbag works.

## 4-86

Boo:  You goin to de Christmas parade dis weekend wit me and de family?

Tib:  Dat sounds good, count me in.  We'll pass a good time no?

Boo:  Yeah, but I'm startin to git sick of dat Santa.  He everywhere now, an why he gots to be so jolly all de time.

Tib:  You would be too if you knew where all de bad girls live.

## 4-87

Boo:  Boy Mah ree was sum mad when we got back from fishin yesterday.

Tib:  Really?  You sed she wuz ok wit us goin?

Boo:  I taught so.  But seems she meant sumting else when she came out de shower yesterday mornin and sed "Tie me up and den do anyting you want."

## 4-88

Boo:  Mah ree done gave me anutter ass chewin dis mornin for sumting I did or didn't do las night.

Tib:  Well life is like a box of chocolates.  You never know watt you goin to git.

Boo:  I thinks it's more like a jar of jalapenos mah fren. Watt you do today just might burn your butt tomorrow.

Boo:  Got an interestin visit from a pretty young lady dis mornin.

Tib:  Really?  Watts dat all bout?

Boo:  Seems de oldest boy wuz at Fred's bar las night, told this little beauty dat his papaw wuz bout to die any day now and leave him ten millon dollars.  He axed her to marry him.

Tib:  So why she came to see you?

Boo:  Seems she wants to marry me.

4-90

Boo:  Hey Tib, lets do dis test dat de daughter bought home las night.  Look at dis here inkblot, watt you see.

Tib:  A naked woman.

Boo:  Hmmm.  How bout dis one.

Tib:  A naked woman lyin in bed.

Boo:  And dis one.

Tib:  A naked woman on her knees.

Boo:  Man Tib, you one sick coonass.

Tib:  Me?  You de one showin me all dem dirty pictures.

4-91

Boo:  You heard bout Comeaux and his truck?

Tib:  I heard he got himsef a new truck.

Boo: Well he built it himsef dis truck. Took de engine from a Chevy, frame from a Ford truck, body from a GMC, transmission from one dem new Toyota Tundra's.

Tib: Really? Watt he end up with?

Boo: Two years.


## 4-92

Boo: Hey Tib, how tall dis here pipe against de shed is you tink?

Tib: Hmmm, lets lay it down here and take a measure wit de tape measure now...It's 24 feet.

Boo: Tib you dummy. I axed for de height, not length.


## 4-93

Boo: I see dat Stephen Hawkings guy done went on his first date in a decade. Paper sez he came back all busted up, broken glasses, broken arm, twisted knee.

Tib: Dat poor guy. Must have been stood up.


## 4-94

Boo: I'm pretty sure de Bordelon's bull is dead down de bayou.

Tib: How you know dat?

Boo: I pissed in it's ear.

Tib: You did watt?

Boo: You know. I leaned over to de bull's ear and sed "Psst". Well it didn't stir an inch so he's got to be dead.

## 4-95

Boo: Dats sum nice floral arrangement you got for your girl dare.

Tib: Tanks, dare tulips. Do you know watts your Mah ree's favorite flower?

Boo: Pretty sure Pillsbury I think.

## 4-96

Tib: So watt you gettin everyone for Christmas?

Boo: Well I bought myself one dem new iPhones. Den I got one dem iPads for de oldest daughter for her school. I got one dem iPod Touches for de oldest son.

Tib: Watt bout Mah ree, watt you got for de wife.

Boo: I got her an iRon.

## 4-97

Boo: Man you wouldn't believe watt dat crazy Latiolais down de bayou be up to.

Tib: Watts dat?

Boo: I well I stops by his camp and I finds him sittin on de toilet wit his fishin pole. He wuz baitin and tossin his hook into de tub.

Tib:  You kiddin me no?  Why you didn't call for a doctor or sumting?

Boo:  I didn't have no time.  I wuz too busy cleanin de fish.


## 4-98

Boo:  Well Mah ree and I are tinkin of takin a vacation to one dem ski resorts after Christmas.

Tib:  Really?  I would tink dat de mountain air might disagree wit Mah ree.

Boo:  Oh it wouldn't dare.


## 4-99

Boo:  Well de oldest son done started his own business on a shoestring.  Done tripled his investment in a week it seems.

Tib:  Tripled?  Wow dats pretty good no?

Boo:  Watts he goin to do wit 3 shoestrings.


## 4-100

Boo:  Heard dat ol man Saucier is marryin himself a 20 year old girl from down de bayou?

Tib:  Ol man Saucier be 70 plus years old no.

Boo:  Yes.  And de little girl wants to have children too.

Tib:  Oh I tink his parents won't let him.

Boo:  Parents?

Tib:  Yes.  Mother Nature and Father Time.

4-101

Boo:  I'm wonderin if I should git a divorce?

Tib:  Why would you do dat?

Boo:  Well Mah ree hasn't spoken to me for six months.

Tib:  Mah fren.  Wives like dat are hard to find.

## A little lagniappe 1

Boo:  Mah ree told me she wants sum new stockins for Christmas but I don't know nuttin bout stockins.

Tib:  Sheer?

Boo:  No.  She's out doin groceries.

## A little lagniappe 2

Boo:  Well de littlest boy been watchin way too much TV. Sed he wanted a box of Tampax for Christmas.

Tib:  Tampax?  You kiddin me?

Boo:  No.  I axed him why and he sed dat wit Tampax you can go swimmin, horseback ridin, skatin anytime you want.

## A little lagniappe 3

Boo:  Hey Tib.  When you and de family come over for de Christmas dinner, you just kick open de front door wit your foot to come in.

Tib:  Why you want me to kick your door in?

Boo:  Surely you won't be comin empty handed.

## A little lagniappe 4

Boo:  Dey ran out of holy water at mass today.  Wonder how dey makes it anyway?

Tib:  Boil de hell out of it.

Boo:  De littlest one noticed dat I be havin sum grey hair now.  She axed me why I got dem.  I told her dat wuz because ever time she wuz bad, I would git a grey hair.

Tib:  Not bad.  So watt she say?

Boo:  She smiled den sed "I guess dats why Pa Paw's hair is all grey".

## 5-1

Boo:  I tried to get an appointment wit de doctor bout dis sore throat I been havin.  Dey can't see me for two weeks.

Tib:  Two weeks?

Boo:  Dat's right.  I sed to dem, I could be dead by den.

Tib:  Dat didn't help?

Boo:  Dey said if dat happened, for me to make sure Mah ree cancels my appointment.

## 5-2

Boo:  Man can you believe de new health care changes we got comin in de new year.

Tib:  Yeah, if you tink it wuz expensive now, wait till it's free.

Boo:  Dey couldn't just leave it alone could dey.

Tib:  Well dats de government for you, if it ain't broke, fix it till it is.

## 5-3

Boo:  Oh Tib, watt happen to your face?

Tib:  A bad case of seenus.

Boo:  Seenus?  You mean Sinus?

Tib:  No seenus.  I was lippin on Mrs. Tassin last night at Fred's bar when Mr. Tassin seen us.

Boo: Brought de oldest boy to see Father Mike today. Axed him to pray for de boy's hearin.

Tib: Did it help?

Boo: Oh don't know, it's not till next week.

## 5-5

Tib: Happy New Year Boo. A nutter year has done gone by, and a nutter year of marriage. Watt been your secret for a long and happy marriage?

Boo: Well when Mah ree and me first got married, I set her straight and sed dat I would make all de major decisions and she would make all de little ones.

Tib: So no major decisions made so far?

Boo: Nope, not a one.

## 5-6

Boo: Lets have a nutter beer mah fren.

Tib: Sounds good to me but why you keeps lookin at someting in your pocket after each beer.

Boo: Oh dats a picture of my Mah ree. When she starts to lookin really good, I'll be ready to go home.

## 5-7

Boo: What time it is Tib?

Tib:  Depends on who's askin.

Boo:  I 'm askin.

Tib:  In dat case, de big hand is on de six and...


## 5-8

Boo:  Man I wuz up all night last night, couldn't fall asleep.

Tib:  Did you try countin de sheep?

Boo:  Funny you say dat.  I did try dat.

Tib:  It didn't work?

Boo:  No.  I made a mistake countin den I wuz up all night tryin to find it.


## 5-9

Tib:  You got one fine woman dare Boo?

Boo:  Tanks, she was definitely Mrs. Right.

Tib:  Yes sir.

Boo:  Of course I didn't know her first name wuz goin to be "Always".


## 5-10

Boo:  Had a little bit of accident dis mornin in de truck.

Tib:  Really?  Watt happened?

Boo:  Well I comes round dis turn and dis lady rides by and yells "Pig!" at me.  Well I yell "B@#$h!" back at her.

Tib:  Den watt?

Boo:  Den I ran into one of Plauche's pigs dat wuz out in de middle of de road.


## 5-11

Boo:  Well Mah ree sure was sum pissed at me las night after you and I left Fred's bar axin me why I came home half drunk.

Tib:  Watt you say to her.

Boo:  Dat we ran out of money.


## 5-12

Boo:  De wife started naggin me as soon as I walked in de front door after leavin Tullos's Cotton Bowl party last night.

Tib:  Dats cuz you made her chain too long.


## 5-13

Boo:  Dat wuz an interestin weddin no?

Tib:  Yeah.  I tink de bride wuz second cousin to de groom.

Boo:  So dat splains why one side of de church wuz empty den.

Boo:  Dees doctors, I'm confused by dare names.  Watts dis general practitioner?

Tib:  Dats a doctor dat knows less and less bout more and more till he don't know nuttin bout everyting.

Boo:  Watts a specialist?

Tib:  Dats a doctor dat knows more and more bout less and less till he knows everyting bout nuttin.

Boo:  Den watts a pathologist?

Tib:  Dats a doctor dat knows everyting bout everyting but it's too late.

Boo:  Hey Tib, why you honk at me and make me pull over de side of de road here?

Tib:  I wanted to tell you dat you got a broke out taillight on your truck, see here...

Boo:  Oh no.

Tib:  Hey it's not dat bad, just a broken taillight lens dats all.

Boo:  Not dat.  Where's my bateau and my trailer?

Boo:  I wuz helpin de youngest wit her alphabet las night.

Tib:  How she did?

Boo:  Pretty good till I axes her what comes after "I".

Tib:  Watt she say?

Boo:  "Yi yi".

Tib:  Listen to dis.  Dares dis cow, dis ant, and an ol fart.  Dey be talkin bout who is greatest of de tree of dem.  De cow sez she is cuz she gives four gallons of milk every day.  De ant sez he is cuz is always be workin and can carry 50 times his weight.

Boo:  So watts de ol fart say?

Tib:  You tell me.

Boo:  I shot dat buck at 600 yards today.

Mah ree:  I guess dats far, I can't picture it though.

Boo:  Dats like 6 football fields.

Mah ree:  Nope.  Dat don't help.

Boo:  Picture two super Walmarts.

Mah ree:  Wow dat far.

Boo:  You mind if I bring my dog wit me to stay at your camp down de bayou?

Tib: You know. I've never had a dog drink all my beer, or eat my fridge empty, or chase my women. Of course he can come.

Boo: Dats great.

Tib: Now if de dog can vouch for you, you're welcome too.

## 5-20

Tib: Man I had a good night sleep down here at de huntin camp las night.

Boo: Not me, why you waked me up and den kissed me on my cheek and sed we we're goin to have a good time? I wuz up rest of de night watchin you after dat.

Tib: Stopped your snorin didn't it.

## 5-21

Tib: Got my weekly staff meetin at plant dis mornin. I hate dem cuz it takes forever, can't git no work done.

Boo: Well our manager has our weekly staff meetin for every Friday at 4:30.

Tib: Right before de weekend?

Boo: Dats right. At dat time, nobody be axin questions.

## 5-22

Boo: I'm goin in to git sum coffee, how bout you Tib?

Tib: Dat sounds good, I'll take sum witout cream.

Boo: Hmmm, I don't tinks we have cream, will you take it witout milk?

### 5-23

Tib: Watts de matter Boo? You looks confused lookin at dem frozen turkeys dare.

Boo: Well Mah ree sed for me to fry de male one but I can'ts tell de differance.

Tib: Which ones got de tv remote?

### 5-24

Boo: Hey Tib, I just saw sum guys drive off in your truck.

Tib: Oh no! Did you try to stop dem?

Boo: I couldn't stop em but don't worry mah fren, I gots de license plate number.

### 5-25

Boo: I tink I can say dat I'm fully committed to de computer age in my house now.

Tib: How you know dat?

Boo: Cuz I can't remember de last time I played solitaire wit real cards.

### 5-26

Mah ree: Boo, let's go out and have sum fun tonight.

Boo:  Dat sounds good.  Since you be probably gettin home fore I do, leave de porch light on for me.


## 5-27

Tib:  Nice weddin las night no?

Boo:  Yep, dat wuz a real nice one, happy couple.

Tib:  I wonderin why de bride always be wearin white.

Boo: I t's a good idea to have dishwasher match de stove and fridge no?


## 5-28

Boo:  How bout a cup of Mah ree's coffee?

Tib:  Mah ree's?  No tanks.

Boo:  I know.  Tirty years of marriage and dat woman make's de worse coffee.

Tib:  I think you might have de "grounds" for divorce dare.


## 5-29

Boo:  Oh my Mah ree sum mad at me dis mornin for bein out so late wit you last night.  But you know, I have a clear conscience bout it all.

Tib:  Don't member a thing do you?

Boo:  Nope.

Tib:  Hey Boo, pull yourself up to de bar here and have a shake wit me.

Boo:  Aarghh, it's tough climbin up on dis stool here.  I tink I'll have a banana split.

Tib:  Crushed nuts?

Boo:  Oh no, just my arthritis.

Boo:  Dang it!  We havin no luck wit de fishin today.

Tib:  Cuz it's windy.

Boo:  Huh, no it's Thursday.

Tib: S o am I, start up de boat and lets go have a beer.

Boo:  Whoa check out de babe at de end of de bar dare.

Tib:  Ai yi yiii.

Boo:  Why don't you go buy her a beer?

Tib:  Nope can't do dat.

Boo:  Why not?

Tib:  Cuz I would be jealous of de bottle.

## 5-33

Tib:  Watts you and Mah ree's secret to makin yalls marriage last so?

Boo:  Well two times a week we go have a nice dinner and few beers.

Tib:  Really?  I never seen yall out at dinner?

Boo:  She goes on Tuesday, I go on Fridays wit you.

## 5-34

Boo:  Man went to de Winn Dixie last night and when you walk by de veggies, it thunders and rains on dem.  When you walk by de milk, you hear mooin.  Go by de eggs, you hear chickens. Walk by de meat you smell charcoal grillin.  Ain't dat sumting?

Tib:  I don't buy toilet paper dare no more.

## 5-35

Tib:  Man Boo! Can you believe de size of all dees chickens in dis Walmart.  I need sum bigger chickens for de bar b que.

Boo:  Yep, dey are a bit small.

Tib:  I wondered ifin I should axe someone here if dey git any bigger.

Boo:  Well I'd say no cuz all dees chickens are dead.

Tib:  So did you sendin in a photo of 4 twenties to de sheriff take care of your speedin ticket?

Boo:  Well since dey took a picture of me speedin and gave me a ticket, I taught I could send dem a picture too but de sheriff's reply changed my mind and I sent de real money in.

Tib:  Watt he say?

Boo:  Didn't say nuttin.  He sent me back a picture of handcuffs.


## 5-37

Tib:  See dat looker at de end of de bar dare?

Boo:  Whoa, yes a looker she is.

Tib:  I went to talk to her before you got here.  She told me she will screw anybody, anytime, anywhere.  She sed my place, her place, it didn't matter.  Been doin it since she got out of college and loves it.

Boo:  Wow, so why you still here?

Tib:  Don't much care for lawyers.


## 5-38

Tib:  Las night dare wuz dis babe at Fred's bar.  She sneezed and her glass eye shot out across de bar and I caught it.  Well she comes over and tanks me den buys me drinks den takes me home.  Wild night den she even cooked breakfast for me.

Boo:  Wow.  You tink she does dat for every guy she meets?

Tib:  Oh no.  I just happen to catch her eye.

Boo:  Barkeep, bring us a shot of tequila.

Tib:  Oh not for me, I don't know how you drink dat stuff.

Boo:  But it's good for you.

Tib: Really?  See dat dead worm at bottom of de bottle dare, watts dat tell ya?

Boo:  Dat I won't be gettin worms.

Boo:  You know Tib, when I wuz a youngster, when my manhood wuz at attention, I couldn't bend it with either hand. In my tirties, I could bend it just slightly, in my forties, a bit more.  Now I can bend it almost half way.

Tib:  Watt you tryin to say?

Boo:  I'm wonderin how much stronger I'm goin to git.

Boo:  Ok Mah ree, here you are wit me at Fred's bar to see watt I've been doin.  Watt you want to drink?

Mah ree:  I guess I'll have watt you have.

Boo:  Ok, two shots of whiskey den.  Here you go cher, drink up.

Mah ree.  Oh gawd, dat's terrible.  I don't see how you drink dat stuff.

Boo:  Dare you go.  And you taught I wuz out here passin a good time when I came here.

## 5-42

Boo: Hey Tib, check out dis frog I got in my pocket.  Found it today.  It sed to me dat it wuz a princess and if I kissed it, she would do anyting for me.

Tib:  Why don't you kiss it den?

Boo:  I don't need no princess.  But a talkin frog is pretty cool.

## 5-43

Tib:  How bout one more beer.

Boo:  You know Tib, dat Tammy Faye Bakker wuz some kind of babe don't you tink.

Tib:  Forget dat beer, time to head home mah fren.

## 5-44

Tib:  Ok Boo, I don't git it.  You been drinkin dem martini's all night and each time you take de olive and put it in dat jar in your pocket.

Boo:  Dats right, and it's almost full.

Tib:  Why you doin dat?

Boo:  Well my Mah ree sent me out for a jar of olives.

## 5-45

Tib:  I got to lose sum weight and de doctor put me on dis diet where I eats whatever I want for two days den skip a day and den start all over.  Sez I should lose 5 pounds in 2 weeks.

Boo: Oh no. No way I could do dat diet.

Tib: Why not?

Boo: Doin dat skippin all day on de turd day would kill me.


### 5-46

Boo: Man dats crazy stuff happenin in Egypt no? I'm gettin all kinds of emails not axin me for money.

Tib: Oh don't be sendin no money dare?

Boo: Why not?

Tib: Probably some "pyramid" scheme.


### 5-47

Mah ree: Boo you know de Trahan's next door?

Boo: Of course.

Mah ree: Well every mornin when Mr. Trahan leaves for work, he gives his wife a big kiss goodbye. How come you never do dat?

Boo: Well Mah ree, I don't know Mrs. Trahan dat well.


### 5-48

Mah ree: Oh Boo, I just dreamed you gave me 500 dollars to buy whatever I want. You wouldn't be spoilin my dream would you cher?

Boo: Oh no, you may keep de 500 dollars my dear.

5-49

Tib: Looks like you got a knot on de back of your head, how dat happen?

Boo: Well I wuz sittin with de littlest one last night, she wantin to look through our old weddin album. Den she sees de picture of Mah ree in her weddin dress. She sez "Is dat when momma came to work for us?". I guess I shouldn't have laughed so loud wit Mah ree right behind us.


5-50

Boo: Ifin my oldest boy had just half a brain, he could get a job and be out de house by now.

Tib: Bein a bit harsh on de boy aren't we?

Boo: You know you're right Tib, if he had even half a brain he'd be gifted.


5-51

Tib: I heard dat poor ole Latour had heart attack and died on you while yall were playin golf yesterday.

Boo: Dats right. Poor ting, just keeled over on de ninth hole. Lambert and I had to carry him all de way back to de club house.

Tib: Dat must have worn yall out.

Boo: Carryin him wasn't bad but puttin him down den pickin him up for every shot wore us out.

Boo:  De wife and I got to arguin, I mean a "discussion" last night.  Den she got all historical on me.

Tib:  You mean hysterical no?

Boo:  No I mean historical, she kept bringin up de past.

Boo:  Boy fixin my truck ended up costin a lot to get out de shop.

Tib:  Underestimated no?

Boo:  No, it wuz just more den I taught it would be.

Boo:  Almost tax time agin.  Man I hate payin dose taxes.

Tib: Y ou got to pay your taxes wit a smile mah fren.

Boo:  I tried dat.  Dey want money.

Tib:  Paper sez dat Colorado has over 100 thousand cattle guards.  Can you believe dat.

Boo:  100 thousand?  Why would dey need dat many.  Dey should fire at least half of dem and save sum state money right dare.

Tib:  You know Boo, we be gettin dat age where we need to be tinkin bout de hearafter.

Boo:  Oh I tink bout it many times a day.

Tib:  Really?

Boo:  Yes, just did mornin I did.  I walked out to de truck and den I wuz sayin to myself, "Now watt wuz I here after?".

Boo:  Let's head over to Fred's bar, I hear dey gots dis new whiskey dare called Viagra.

Tib:  Well lets go pour ourselves a stiff one den.

Boo:  Hey Tib, you tink you can jump higher den dat fence?

Tib:  I know I can.

Boo:  I bet you twenty you can't.  Let's see, now jump.

Tib:  Ok, here I go.

Boo:  Ha!  You might have jumped a foot in de air.  You lose.

Tib:  Wait, de fence hasn't had a chance to jump yet.

5-59

Tib:  Ok Boo, we been here drinkin at Fred's bar all night wit you havin a pair of underwear on your head.  Watts up wit dat?

Boo:  I decided to wear dem on my head on Thursday when drinkin.

Tib:  Really?  But today is Wednesday.

Boo:  Oh gawd I must really look stupid.


5-60

Boo:  Last night I was teachin de youngest one's bout de ten commandments.  I told dem my favorite one wuz "honor thy father and thy mother".  So dey axes me if dare be a commandment bout how to treat sons and daughters.  I sed dare wuzn't one.

Tib:  Dare is one.

Boo:  Really?

Tib:  Sure.  "Thou shalt not kill."


5-61

Boo:  My girl in high school told me sumting funny bout one of her classmates at school today. Seems dis classmate is one dem Arab boys goin to school over here.  He drives dis fancy Merecedes to school.  He wrote his papaw back in Saudi dat he wuz embarrassed to drive his Mercedes when all his classmates came in buses.

Tib:  So watt de father do?

Boo: Bought him a bus.


## 5-62

Tib:  Boo, let me put dat key in for you, you be too drunk to do it.

Boo:  I got it, just give me a nutter try.

Tib:  Come on Boo, I don't have all night waitin to see if you git inside.  You can't keep de key steady.

Boo:  I'm holdin de key steady.  You grab hold of de house and I'll git dis time.


## 5-63

Boo:  I sure do admire my new boss at de plant.

Tib:  And why?

Boo:  Cuz if I don't, he'd fire me.


## 5-64

Boo:  Man I need to get one dem physical check ups for me and Mah ree, we gettin old you know and we need to start doin dat.  But it's just so expensive.

Tib:  Well if you can't afford it, just go to de airport.  Dey do free x-rays and breast exams right dare.

Boo:  Ha, dats true, but I need one dem colon check ups too.

Tib:  Dats easy, just say two words to get dat.

Boo:  Watt two words?

Tib:  Al Qaeda.


## 5-65

Tib:  You tink you're a optimist or a pessimist?

Boo:  Watt de difference?

Tib:  Well a optimist tinks de glass is half full and de pessimist tinks it's half empty.

Boo:  Hmmm, well I guess dat depends den?

Tib:  On watt?

Boo:  Who has to wash de glass.


## 5-66

Boo:  Doctor sed I had high blood pressure.  I sed it ran in my family.

Tib:  Dats so.  Which side?

Boo:  On Mah ree's side.

Tib:  Now dat can't be Boo.

Boo:  Watt you mean, you met her family before, dey would drive anyone's blood pressure up.


## 5-67

Boo:  Mah ree put me on de phone wit her mamaw and she talked my ear off all night.

Tib: You need to recommend dat she go to one dem self help groups.

Boo: Which one is dat?

Tib: On and on anon.


## 5-68

Tib: So how wuz your trip wit Mah ree to de casino.

Boo: Pretty good till Mah ree fainted.

Tib: Watt happened?

Boo: Well she got tired of watchin me play blackjack so I told her to go bet on de roulette wheel. She didn't know watt number so I sed bet it on her age. Well she put all her money down and dey spent the wheel. When it stopped, she fainted?

Tib: It hit her age, 49?

Boo: Yep, but she bet on 39.


## 5-69

Boo: Dang it, I'm tired of my Mah ree bein on my case bout everyting. I can't do nuttin right round here.

Tib: Mah fren, don't you know dat marriage is bout relationship in which one person always be right, and de utter is you, de husband.


## 5-70

Tib: Did you hear dat baby cryin all durin mass yesterday.

Boo:  Sure did.

Tib:  I don't know why dey don't just take dat baby out back.

Boo:  I know, kept wakin me up.

## 5-71

Boo:  Ol papaw is gettin on in years. Wonder how you know it's time to put him in a home?

Tib:  Try dis.  Fill de bathtub wit water.  Den give him a teaspoon, a cup, and a bucket and axes him to empty de tub.

Boo:  Hmmm, I would use de bucket.

Tib:  A normal person would plug de plug.  Do you want a bed near a window?

## 5-72

Tib:  Check out dis tombstone.

Boo:  "Here lies a lawyer and a honest man."  Ok, watts so special bout dat.

Tib:  Since when dey start buryin two people in one grave?

## 5-73

Boo:  Sez here in de paper dat President Obama wants to rename dat fault line dat runs through Baton Rouge.

Tib:  Let me guess, change it to Bush's Fault right.

Boo:  Man dis some good wine no?

Tib:  Dis sure is.

Boo:  Which would you give up ifin you had to, women or wine?

Tib:  Dat depends on de age mah fren.

Tib:  I see you got two crawfish growin in dat fishbowl dare.

Boo:  De youngest one wants to grow dem.  Named on of dem "One" and de utter "Two".

Tib:  Why she name dem dat?

Boo:  She sed cuz if one died, she'd still have two.

Boo:  How wuz dat girl you left wit from Fred's bar last night.

Tib:  De one dat looked like Cindi Crawford right.

Boo:  Yeah, dats right!

Tib:  Well den you had too much to drink too.  Dis mornin she looked more like Broderick Crawford.

5-77

Boo:  Man I just can't sleep knowin I cheated on my taxes so I'm goin to write a check to de IRS for $100 and send it to dem.

Tib:  Dats all you cheated dem?

Boo:  Oh no, far from it, but if I still can't sleep, I might send de rest.


5-78

Boo:  Check out de pair of babes over dare.

Tib:  I went and talked to dem before you came in.

Boo:  How did it go?

Tib:  Well I axed dem "where dey were from" and one of dem laughed at me and sed "Where we come from people don't end dare sentences wit a preposition."

Boo:  Ouch, watt you sed to dat?

Tib:  I sed "Where you from B@#$&?"


5-79

Boo:  Did you watch dat show bout Eskimos on Discovery las night?

Tib:  Pretty cold weather up dare no?

Boo:  In dem fur suits all de time, I wonder how dey make babies?

Tib:  Dey keep rubbin dare noses together till de little boogers come out.

166

## 5-80

Boo: De credit card company called me today bout my oldest daughter's credit card bein stolen.

Tib: Stolen? When?

Boo: Oh bout a month ago.

Tib: A month? Why you didn't call de credit card people earlier?

Boo: De thief be spendin less den de daughter ever did.


## 5-81

Tib: Man dats sum kind of nice thermos you brought wit you fishin today.

Boo: Dat it is, keepin my hot stuff hot and keepin my cold stuff cold.

Tib: Watt you got in it now?

Boo: Four cups of coffee and a ice cream bar.


## 5-82

Boo: Ran into our old buddy Gauthier dis mornin.

Tib: Dat rascal, how he's doin?

Boo: Not bad but sez his boy tinks he's a chicken.

Tib: A chicken? Why he don't bring him to a doctor?

Boo: Sez he needs de eggs.

Tib: Nice weddin for de nephew no? Dey say a man is incomplete till he is married.

Boo: Dats true. Den he's finished.

Boo: Las night I read bout de evils of drinkin.

Tib: So watt you goin to do den.

Boo: Give up readin.

Boo: Dat is sum nice truck you got dare Tib.

Tib: Yes it is mah fren.

Boo: I bet it's fast no?

Tib: So fast dat de payments are 3 months behind.

Boo: You see dat Aucoin boy done graduated from college and opened him up a vetenary clinic and taxidermy down de bayou. Strange combination don't cha tink?

Tib: Not really. Either way, you git your pet back.

# 5-87

Tib:  Watch dis Boo, I'm goin to show you de harmful effects of drinkin whiskey right here.  See dis can I put sum fishin worms here.  See dem squirmin round.  Now watch watt happens when I pour some Jack Daniels in de can.

Boo:  Whoa!  Dey all curled up and died.

Tib:  So watts dat tell you.

Boo:  Dat we won't never have worms.

# 5-88

Tib:  Watcha readin dare?

Boo:  It's my marriage certificate.

Tib:  You been married tirty some years, watcha lookin for?

Boo:  An expiration date.

# 5-89

Boo:  Heard Hebert's wife got killed by dare mule yesterday? Kicked her in de head.

Tib:  Dats a shame.

Boo:  Wonder how much he wants for dat mule?

Tib:  Sameting came cross my mind.

Tib:  Hey Boo, I tink it's time to head home.  De wife not goin to appreciate you gettin home half drunk you know.

Boo:  Well I'm soooo sorry.  She could have given me more money den.

Boo:  Ok, I go to mass every Sunday, dats goin to get me into heaven you tink?

Tib:  Nope.

Boo:  Say I sell everyting I got includin my dear bateau over dare and gave it all to de church.  Would dat get me into heaven?

Tib:  Nope.

Boo:  Den how am goin to get to heaven?

Tib:  You gotta be dead.

Boo:  Dees kids today shore like dis "rap" music dees days. Wonder why dey call it rap music.

Tib:  De letter "c" fell off at de printers.

Tib:  Sumbody gave me a big ole jar of prunes yesterday.

Boo:  Dey always give you a good run for de money.

Tib:  Can you believe dat Monica Lewinsky girl be almost 40 now.

Boo:  Seems just like yesterday she wuz foolin round wit Clinton.

Tib:  Watt you tink you would have sed after bein caught like Clinton?

Boo:  Oh I wouldn't have gotten to say nuttin. I would have been layin in pool of my own blood lookin up at Mah ree reloadin de shotgun.

Tib:  Dat wuz one good dinner at Fred's tonight no?

Boo:  I guess so.  It wuz kind of like bein married.

Tib:  How goin to restaurant wit friends like bein married?

Boo:  Well you order what you want den when you see what de utters got, you wish you had dat.

Boo:  Got called in to teacher's office for de youngest boy. Seems de teacher didn't like his answer.

Tib:  Watt wuz de question?

Boo:  She axed him who shot Abraham Lincoln and he sed he didn't.

Tib: Really?

Boo:  Look Tib, ifin my boy sed he didn't do it, he didn't do it.

## 5-97

Boo:  Today I was drivin down de lane near Savoy's farm when my truck stopped.  I wuz lookin under de hood when one of Savoy's cows came up to me and sed "It's probably de carborator."

Tib:  Really?  Dats incredible.

Boo:  Watts incredible, stupid cow, it wasn't de carborator.  I wuz out of gas.

## 5-98

Boo:  Seems de restaurant bizness of Fred's bar not doin so good.

Tib:  I tink it's de new smokin law, people don't want to eat wit smoke all round.

Boo:  Well de bar part is de only smokin section?

Tib:  Havin a smokin section in a restaurant is like havin a peeing section in a swimmin pool.

## 5-99

Boo:  Man I hate payin de IRS dis time of year.

Tib:  You ever notice when you put "The" and "IRS" together.

Boo:  THEIRS?

Tib:  Dats right.

## 5-100

Boo:  I love you.

Mah ree:  Dats nice Boo.  Is dat you or de beer talkin?

Boo:  Dats me...talkin to de beer.


## 5-101

Tib:  Watt you tinks is more important, de moon or de sun.

Boo:  Hmmm, I'm sayin de moon.

Tib:  Moon?  Whys dat?

Boo:  Well de moon gives us light at night time.

Tib:  Well de sun does gives light too?

Boo:  But dats durin de daytime when we don't need it.

# A little lagniappe 1

Boo:  De wife had plastic surgery last night.

Tib:  Really?

Boo:  Dats right.  I cut up her credit cards.

# A little lagniappe 2

Tib:  Boo, why you paintin your sun dial wit dat fluorescent paint?

Boo:  Dats so I will be able to tell de time at night.

Tib:  Ok Boo.  You got a right to be stupid but now you be abusin dat privilege.

# A little lagniappe 3

Tib:  Hey dare Boo, I see you got a bag of donuts dare.  If I guess how many you got, will you give me one.

Boo:  Tell you watt Tib.  If you guess de right number, I'll give you boat of dem.

# A little lagniappe 4

Boo:  I decided I would go wit Mah ree to her aerobics class last night.  I tell you I bent, twisted, gyrated, jumped up and down, I sweated for an hour.

Tib:  So how wuz de class?

Boo:  Dat wuz to git into de gym shorts.  By de time I got dem on, de class wuz over.

## A little lagniappe 5

Tib:  How long you been happily married now?

Boo:  Ten years.

Tib:  Your oldest is almost twenty, watt you mean ten years?

Boo:  You sed happily married.  Happily married ten out of 25 is not bad no.


## A little lagniappe 6

Boo:  I gots to lose some weight, I'm getting too big in de waist area.

Tib:  Well you know dat sayin.

Boo:  Watt sayin.

Tib:  De waist is a terrible ting to mind.

Keep an eye out for the next Down de Bayou Boo and Tib jokes book coming soon on your friendly Kindle / Amazon website.

Made in the USA
Coppell, TX
23 July 2020